Bloom's
GUIDES

Ernest Hemingway's
The Sun Also Rises

The Adventures of Huckleberry Finn
All the Pretty Horses
Animal Farm
Beloved
Beowulf
Brave New World
The Catcher in the Rye
The Chosen
The Crucible
Cry, the Beloved Country
Death of a Salesman
Fahrenheit 451
Frankenstein
The Glass Menagerie
The Grapes of Wrath
Great Expectations
The Great Gatsby
Hamlet
The Handmaid's Tale
The House on Mango Street
I Know Why the Caged Bird Sings
The Iliad
Jane Eyre

Lord of the Flies
Macbeth
Maggie: A Girl of the Streets
The Member of the Wedding
The Metamorphosis
Native Son
Of Mice and Men
1984
The Odyssey
Oedipus Rex
One Hundred Years of Solitude
Pride and Prejudice
Ragtime
The Red Badge of Courage
Romeo and Juliet
Slaughterhouse-Five
The Scarlet Letter
Snow Falling on Cedars
A Streetcar Named Desire
The Sun Also Rises
A Tale of Two Cities
The Things They Carried
To Kill a Mockingbird
The Waste Land

Bloom's
GUIDES

Ernest Hemingway's
The Sun Also Rises

Edited & with an Introduction
by Harold Bloom

BLOOM'S
LITERARY CRITICISM
An imprint of Infobase Publishing

Bloom's Guides: The Sun Also Rises

Copyright © 2007 Infobase Publishing

Introduction © 2007 by Harold Bloom

Bloom's Literary Criticism
An imprint of Infobase Publishing
132 West 31st Street
New York NY 10001

ISBN-10: 0-7910-9359-X
ISBN-13: 978-0-7910-9359-7

Library of Congress Cataloging-in-Publication Data
Ernest Hemingway's The sun also rises / Harold Bloom, editor.
    p. cm. — (Bloom's guides)
    Includes bibliographical references (p.   ) and index.
    ISBN 0-7910-9359-X
    1. Hemingway, Ernest, 1899-1961. Sun also rises. [1. American literature—History and criticism.] I. Bloom, Harold. II. Title: Sun also rises. III. Series.
    PS3515.E37S8 2007
    813'.52--dc22   2006037267

Contributing Editor: Portia Williams Weiskel
Cover design by Takeshi Takahashi
Printed in the United States of America
Bang EJB 10 9 8 7 6 5 4 3 2 1
This book is printed on acid-free paper.

Contents

Introduction 7

Biographical Sketch 10

The Story Behind the Story 13

List of Characters 16

Summary and Analysis 20

Critical Views

The New York Times Book Review of *The Sun Also Rises*
(1926) 49

Carlos Baker on Hemingway's Skill at Telling It
"The Way It Was" 51

Mark Spilka on the Ruination of "the good place" 54

Philip Young on the Novel as Hemingway's *Waste Land* 57

Donald Daiker on Jake's Achievement of Self-Mastery 59

Mimi Reisel Gladstein on Brett as Hemingway's
Destructive Indestructible Woman 64

Scott Donaldson on Bill Gorton's Humor 69

Robert Casillo on the Ostracism of Robert Cohn 73

Thomas Strychacz on Jake as Observer 74

Peter Griffin on the Models for Jake and Brett 76

James Nagel on the Other Women 77

Debra A. Moddelmog on Sexual Ambiguity in the Novel 81

Linda Wagner-Martin on Henry James's Influence
in the Novel 86

Works by Ernest Hemingway 93

Annotated Bibliography 95

Contributors 101

Acknowledgments 104

Index 107

 Introduction

HAROLD BLOOM

So severely stylized and rigorously mannered is Ernest Hemingway's *The Sun Also Rises* that it continues to achieve a classic status, decades after its initial publication. It is a masterpiece of stance and of sensibility, and like *The Great Gatsby* (which influenced it) *The Sun Also Rises* evades all the dangers that might have reduced it to become another mere period piece. Again like *The Great Gatsby*, *The Sun Also Rises* is something of a prose-poem, emerging from the literary era dominated by T. S. Eliot's *The Waste Land*. Like Eliot himself, who was much affected by Joseph Conrad's *Heart of Darkness*, both Fitzgerald and Hemingway take up a narrative stance that is influenced by Conrad's Marlow, the prime narrator of *Heart of Darkness*, *Lord Jim*, and (though he is unnamed there) "The Secret Sharer." Nick Carraway in *The Great Gatsby* and Jake Barnes in *The Sun Also Rises* are equivocal narrators, each with a protagonist who is his main concern: Gatsby for Carraway, and Lady Brett Ashley for Jake Barnes. There is something feminine in sensibility about both Carraway and Barnes, as there was about Conrad's Marlow, and about Eliot's Tiresias, the implied narrative sensibility of *The Waste Land*.

The wounded Fisher King of *The Waste Land*, impotent and yearning for spiritual salvation, is clearly akin to the impotent Jake Barnes, maimed in World War I and so no longer Brett Ashley's lover, though they continue to be in love with one another. Interpreters of Brett take remarkably varied views of her, ranging from a man-eating, Circean bitch-goddess to another lost Waste Lander, stoic and disinterested and essentially tragic, questing for what cannot be recovered, a lost image of sexual fulfillment. It is suggestive that the hidden model for Eliot's *The Waste Land* was the most powerful of all American poems, Walt Whitman's elegy for the martyred Abraham Lincoln, *When Lilacs Last in the Dooryard Bloom'd*.

Whitman's poem is truly a self-elegy, as are *The Waste Land*, *The Great Gatsby*, and *The Sun Also Rises*. When the funeral procession of President Lincoln passes him, Whitman makes a symbolic gesture of self-castration by surrendering the "tally," the sprig of lilac that was his own image of voice, and more ambiguously the image for his sexual identity. Elegy is the literary genre of *The Sun Also Rises* and ought to help determine our attitude towards Brett as well as towards Jake, who mourns not only his lost potency but his largely abandoned Catholicism.

Hemingway's nostalgias were numerous: for God, heroism, a perfect love, and an antagonistic supremacy in Western literature, even against such titans as Melville and Tolstoy. *The Sun Also Rises* profoundly studies many other American nostalgias but above all our longing for innocence, in the Whitmanian sense of an original American destiny, compounded of freedom, hope, and millennial potential. Against that "optative mood," as Ralph Waldo Emerson termed it, Hemingway sets the negativity of Ecclesiastes, the most nihilistic book of the Hebrew Bible. The novel's epigraph, the source of its title, states Hemingway's ethos and also the stoic condition of Jake Barnes and Brett Ashley:

> One generation passeth away, and another generation cometh; but the earth abideth forever.... The sun also ariseth, and the sun goeth down, and hasteth to the place where he arose.... The wind goeth toward the south, and turneth about unto the north; it whirleth about continually, and the wind returneth again according to his circuits.... All the rivers run into the sea; yet the sea is not full; unto the place from whence the rivers come, thither they return again.

All the generations are lost—not just that of Brett and Jake and their friends—in this dark view of mortality and mutability. *The Sun Also Rises*, like Ecclesiastes, does not urge us either to religious assurance or to an absolute nihilism or despair. One of the most poignant of all American elegies, it affirms the virtues of giving a style to despair and of enduring the loss of love with something like a tragic dignity. Hemingway was never again to write so compelling a novel, though his genius for the short story continued undiminished. Lyrical intensity has rarely sustained a novel with such economy, or such grace.

Biographical Sketch

In his introduction to *Men at War* (1942, p. xv) Hemingway wrote, "A writer's job is to tell the truth." In 1948, with much of his published work behind him, he wrote that truth was "made of knowledge, experience, wine, bread, oil, salt, vinegar, bed, early mornings, nights, days, the sea, men, women, dogs, beloved motor cars, bicycles, hills and valleys, the appearance and disappearance of trains on straight and curved tracks...." These words from a pragmatic sensibility, a mind trained as a journalist to see and record objectively, also reveal a love for the details of nature and daily life.

Hemingway was born (July 21, 1899) into comfortable and privileged circumstances—in the respectable community of Oak Park, Illinois, to a family with means and aspirations—but never allowed himself to be defined by the prevailing expectations. Tellingly, he never wrote about his hometown. Hemingway's biographers emphasize the importance of family summers spent in the northern Michigan woods where hiking, fishing, camping, and hunting provided lasting knowledge and enjoyment of nature. Less well-known is Hemingway's tutelage in the Louis Agassiz tradition which encouraged a naturalist's observation of nature for its own sake but also for gleaning signs of the Creator working His miracles. The sacred and restorative power of nature is ubiquitous in Hemingway's fiction. In *The Sun Also Rises* religious feeling and imagery permeate the brief respite Jake and Bill enjoy fishing in the Irati River.

Instead of the customary trajectory of attending college after high school, Hemingway began work (Summer 1917) as a novice reporter for *The Kansas City Star*. The spare, unprepossessing, and energetic sentences he learned to write as a journalist later became the trademark style of his fiction.

Hemingway's military experience was brief (less than a month) but intense, and it generated legends about his heroism as well as material for his stories. He was famously wounded in Italy (July 8, 1918) while a volunteer for the

American Red Cross, and just as famously fell in love with his nurse during his recuperation in Milan. *A Farewell to Arms* (1929) is his fictional re-creation of this experience. Richard Attenborough's 1996 film *In Love and War* is an imperfect rendering of Hemingway's war experiences. Biographer Carlos Baker writes that Hemingway didn't succumb to the explosion—he absorbed 200 pieces of shrapnel from an Austrian mortar shell—until he had rescued a wounded Italian soldier. Italy honored his heroism with a medal Hemingway prized for the rest of his life.

Back home in 1919 Hemingway appeared in a self-styled uniform similar to those worn by Italian military officers. Such a bold gesture reveals two important traits of his personality: his likely boredom with ordinary life in Oak Park (or anywhere) and his preoccupation with self-image. Hemingway was also influenced by the "Rough Rider" presidency of Teddy Roosevelt (1901–1909) that projected a vigorous masculine image of adventure, daring, service, and honor. Roosevelt's famous words—"Walk softly and carry a big stick"—describe Hemingway's understated and potent writing style.

Restless, bored, and at odds with his mother, Hemingway traveled to Toronto in 1920 to work for the *Toronto Star*. Back in Chicago he met Hadley Richardson, the first of his four wives. They married in 1921. With Hadley's trust fund and Hemingway's foreign correspondent's assignment, they sailed to Europe.

Following the devastation of World War I—"the war [that was to have ended] all wars"—Paris in 1921 was the scene for many disillusioned American expatriates. At home in this ambience, and with letters of introduction in hand from Sherwood Anderson, Hemingway was accepted into the literary circle of Ezra Pound and Gertrude Stein. Hemingway's big-hearted adventuring now included extensive traveling, skiing in the Alps, and attending bullfights in Madrid. His job brought him to dramatic world events, including, in 1922, the Lausanne Peace Conference where he not-very-perspicaciously described upcoming fascist dictator Mussolini as "the biggest bluff in Europe."

Hemingway never settled in one place, but wherever he was, when not writing, he was adventuring, often at great risk. With his second wife he moved in 1928 to Key West, where deep-sea fishing filled the days. A string of accidents and injuries, including two plane crashes, began what plagued him—along with depression and paranoia—the rest of his life. Interludes of big-game hunting on safari began in 1933. In 1936 he covered the Spanish Civil War from Madrid. In 1937 he was on *Time*'s cover. By 1940 he was living with his third wife outside Havana. During WW II Hemingway volunteered his fishing vessel the *Pilar* to patrol the Gulf Stream for German warships and later covered the European theatre for *Collier's*.

A period of unproductive writing and severe physical and mental suffering that included the death in 1951 of his mother ended with the sudden appearance of *The Old Man and the Sea* (1953) which earned him the 1954 Nobel Prize for Literature.

Hemingway's fourth wife accompanied him through his final years of anguish and breakdown. In July 1961 he committed suicide in his home in Idaho. In 1928 his father had died similarly. Of his death, the *Louisville Courier-Journal* wrote, "It is almost as though the Twentieth Century itself has come to a sudden, violent, and premature end" (John Raeburn, *Fame Became of Him: Hemingway as Public Writer*, Indiana University Press, 1984, p. 68).

The Hemingway Society, founded in 1980, established the Hemingway Collection at the JFK Library in Boston. Its biannual publication—*The Hemingway Review*—is mailed to 28 nations.

The Story Behind the Story

Hemingway's *The Sun Also Rises* is among the most widely read and commented upon novels in American literature. Since its initial appearance (on October 22, 1926, selling for two dollars a copy), the novel has generated strong reactions ranging from high praise to alarmed disdain. Hemingway's mother deplored what she regarded as the demoralizing subject matter. Hemingway defended himself (unsuccessfully) in a letter to her—"I am trying ... to get the feeling of the actual life.... You can't do this without putting in the ugly as well as what is beautiful." Some early readers judged *Sun* as nihilistic: a book about nothing with people going nowhere. But Edmund Wilson called it the best novel of Hemingway's time, and most readers recognized Hemingway's powerful and moving delineation of an entire generation whose ideals of love for country, family, and religion had been desecrated by the ravages of World War I. In the figure of Jake Barnes, Hemingway had provided for those facing the rest of their lives with wounded bodies, lost loves, and damaged spirits—not salvation or restoration, but possibility— an alternative way to live with dignity and meaning.

So recognizable was Hemingway's incorporation of people and events from his own experience into his story that international guessing games about identities sprang up. Several accounts of these parallels have been written. (See, for examples, Sheridan Baker's essay in *The Merrill Studies* on *"The Sun Also Rises,"* 1969, and relevant sections in Carlos Baker's *Hemingway: The Writer as Artist*, fourth edition, 1972.) Like Jake Barnes, Hemingway was working as a foreign correspondent while writing the novel. For work and pleasure, he traveled extensively in Europe, and came to respect the qualities he gave to Jake: not those of the tourist, but those of a respectful insider who makes an effort to know the language, customs, people, and geography. Jake is multilingual, savvy about places to go and making reservations to get there, and he has earned the respect of Montoya.

Two significant historical events influenced the novel. In 1920 the Nineteenth Amendment granted suffrage to American women. Post-WW I images of the liberated "new woman" are relevant for understanding both Brett and Frances Clyne. Also the famous "Monkey Trial" of 1925 upheld Creationism and banned John T. Scopes from teaching evolution in Tennessee. Religion and nature are important themes in the novel, figuring most prominently in the trout-fishing scene and the humorous banter between Jake and Bill.

Hemingway left Pamplona in July 1925 and began writing his first novel. It took eight and a half weeks and went through many revisions. (See Frederic Joseph Svoboda's *Hemingway and* The Sun Also Rises, 1983, for a comprehensive study of Hemingway's changes.) *Fiesta* and *Lost Generation* were alternative titles. Originally, the young bullfighter was the hero and all the action was in Spain, but when Hemingway realized he was writing a more complex novel he began the story in Paris and made Jake the central figure. Hemingway was also influenced by F. Scott Fitzgerald's opinion that the first thirty pages were inferior.

Of the novel, Hemingway wrote he intended "...the earth abiding forever as the hero" (*Selected Letters, 1917–1961*, 229). And his epigraph from Ecclesiastes offers the consolation of the earth's recurring cycles and the perfect harmony of natural rhythms. About the second epigraph— "You are all a lost generation," attributed to Gertrude Stein—there has been misunderstanding. Stein was quoting a garage owner who was referring to the general lassitude of his mechanics. According to Hemingway biographer Carlos Baker, it was Stein, not Hemingway who expanded the term to include all the war-weary young men of the current generation. Of labeling the generation "lost" he told Baker in 1951: "I thought beat-up, maybe [deleted] in many ways. But damned if we were lost except for deads, gueules cassées, and certified crazies. Lost, no ... We were a very solid generation...." (Baker, pp 80, 81).

Not falsely romantic or optimistic, *The Sun Also Rises* is about the impermanence of love and the certainty of pain and death. It is also about taking joy in the vibrancy of Paris's streets, good food and drink, companionship, the lovely Basque countryside, and the possibility of living with a new kind of honor.

List of Characters

Both protagonist and narrator, **Jake Barnes** is also the central figure in overlapping circles of friends and colleagues that make up the expatriate community of Paris in the 1920s. A wartime genital wound that destroyed his sexual functioning but—perversely—not his sexual desire now defines much of Jake's postwar life and perspective. Specifically, it prevents consummation with Brett, his onetime nurse and longtime love. Unlike most of the Paris crowd, Jake supports himself with a job (foreign correspondent) and pays attention to deadlines and other responsibilities. Bereft of romantic possibility, Jake chooses to enjoy the non-dramatic, non-heroic pleasures in life—good food, drink, conversation, and trout fishing—and appreciates the heroic passion and skill enacted in the bullfighting festival he attends annually in Spain. Jake's choice—whether or not to introduce Brett to the innocent young bullfighter Romero—is a defining moment for him and provides the pivotal action in the novel.

Just as Jake is not a traditional hero, **Brett Ashley**, English expatriate and former wartime nurse's aide, is not a traditional woman. Despite her mannish short hair and frequent reference to herself as one of "the chaps," Brett's sexual allure for men generates much of the high energy in the novel. She loves one man whom she cannot marry (Jake), is engaged to another whom she does not love (Mike), casually seduces yet another who mistakes her attentions for love (Cohn), and is swept away by a self-indulgent passion for a matador half her age. Wild jealousy, some violence, and a lot of male misbehavior ensue. The war has wounded Brett as grievously as any man; her fiancé died and Jake—her current and long-standing love—has been sexually maimed during his tour of duty. Thus wounded, Brett cultivates an amoral and fun-loving sensibility, and spends much of her time smoking, drinking, and dancing in Parisian nightspots. Her show of independence is perhaps brave but also not quite real. She lives on money from an earlier, abusive marriage and she is "no good at being alone." Her high spirits collapse quickly and often into "misery." Readers interested in feminism and androgyny often focus on Brett's character and behavior.

A published writer and expatriate, **Robert Cohn** is, after Jake, the most complex character in the novel. Partly because he is the only Jew in the expatriate crowd and partly because he lives his life as if it were a romantic adventure, Cohn is never fully accepted, never identified—in Brett's words—as "one of us." Cohn's function in the novel is to portray the sensibility that contrasts with Jake's stoic suffering and that violates Hemingway's code of heroic behavior. His status as one of Brett's numerous rejected suitors is at the center of the escalating sexual tension and violence in the fiesta section of the novel.

In contrast to the amoral ambiance of expatriate life in Paris stands the honor-coded tradition of Spanish bullfighting. **Pedro Romero**, the young matador, represents the ideal of this tradition. Revered and protected by Montoya as one who must remain "incorruptible," Romero allows himself to be seduced by Brett with Jake's help. He functions in the novel as a sexual and heroic surrogate for Jake and as one example (however unrealistic for most people) of how to live with courage and grace in a chaotic postwar world.

Bill Gorton's good-natured and comic sensibility would be wholly praiseworthy if it didn't include the anti-Semitic barbs he aims at Robert Cohn. That this particular bigotry was commonplace, even fashionable, at the time, does not make it acceptable. Without this failing, however, Bill is likeable and unburdened by neurosis or immaturity. He provides Jake and the novel with occasions of playfulness, uncompetitive companionship, and reverence for nature's simple and recurring pleasures. Also an American and a writer, Bill is never smitten with Brett, and is thus the only main male character in Hemingway's story who does not suffer.

The wealthy and jovial **Count Mippipopolous** is a minor character who nonetheless contributes importantly to Hemingway's central concerns. Somewhere in or between his involvement in "seven wars and four revolutions," the Count has sustained two arrow wounds that went "clear through" his abdomen. Although the Count gets some of his wealth from being an absentee owner of a string of sweet shops in America and is extravagant and ostentatious about spending it, his wounds and "hard living" have contributed to a sensibility—a code of values he lives by—that leads Brett to describe him to Jake as "one of us."

Mike Campbell, the perennially drunk upper-class Scot, seems to be the most "lost" of this "lost generation." Family wealth sustains him (he doesn't work) but he is careless about money and frequently near bankruptcy. A brief mention of his having misappropriated another man's war medals suggests a more serious character flaw. Mike is engaged to Brett, but their union is without passion and not interesting.

Montoya, the hotel-keeper in Pamplona, is a minor character but only in the brevity of his appearances. His presence is an essential piece in the moral scaffolding of Hemingway's story. Presiding over the sacred ritual of bullfighting, he has taken on the task of protecting the honor and purity of the up-and-coming bullfighters. Significantly, he has included in his circle one outsider—Jake Barnes—whom he judges an *aficionado*, one with understanding and honorable passion for the art of bullfighting. Montoya's shunning of Jake following the arranged betrayal of young Romero is a measure of Jake's fall from grace and the ironic contamination of his values caused by his doomed love for Brett.

Frances Clyne, Robert Cohn's rejected and desperate girlfriend, and **Georgette**, the prostitute, represent contrasting aspects of Hemingway's conception of love and the female personality. Georgette's profession reduces love and sex to a transient and purchased affair. In conversation with Jake, she introduces the multilayered notion of "sickness" into the novel. Georgette works and is self-sufficient. Frances, having acquired some of the qualities of the new independent woman, is nonetheless possessive, manipulative, and emasculating in her relationship with Cohn. Hemingway did not admire prostitutes, but he looked with complete disdain on women like Frances.

Summary and Analysis

In the section of *The Waste Land* (1922) that T. S. Eliot called "A Game of Chess," two lovers—bored with each other and bored with life—fail even at communicating. One finally says, "What shall we do tomorrow? / What shall we ever do?" Many early readers of *The Sun Also Rises* were struck by the apparent aimlessness of the major characters, as if they too were perennially asking, "What shall we ever do?" and answering by moving on to the next bar. Hemingway had read Eliot's famous poem as well as F. Scott Fitzgerald's *The Great Gatsby* (1925) in which rich and aimless Daisy Buchanan after luncheon one hot summer day frantically asks, "What'll we do with ourselves this afternoon and the day after that, and the next thirty years?"

These characters have in common a sense of loss—of purpose, of meaning, of permanence and connection—that was widely experienced in the West in the years between the two world wars. Hemingway saw that World War I had left many of the postwar generation wounded—if not physically, then emotionally or both. Hemingway himself and his characters, Jake, Mike, Brett, and Count Mippipopolous were all directly touched in one or another way by the ravages of the war. In addition to the personal losses were those more general ones associated with bitter disillusionment: the war officially waged for the grand national purpose of saving democracy turned out to have served less noble interests. Eight million died and millions more were mutilated or paralyzed as a result. Historians record a change in the cultural mood of this period, and it is essential to read Hemingway's story against this backdrop. Hedonism and cynicism were common defenses. So too was alcohol, until the Volstead Act of 1919 established the long reign of Prohibition in America. This deprivation when combined with dismay over the ensuing corruption and rise of reactive organizations like the KKK was enough to drive American intellectuals to Paris where they were known as the expatriates. This is Jake Barnes's community.

Of these expatriates the two least aimless of the group are introduced in Chapters I and II of Book I. Jake's choice of what to tell the reader about Robert Cohn establishes the latter as passive and—despite his Princeton education and success in the literary world—strangely unself-reliant. Cohn's parents' status helps him into college; he "was married by the first girl who was nice to him," who also left him. Later, "he fell among literary people." We learn that Cohn has been ensnared ("taken in hand") by Frances Clyne, his current lady, who frustrates his effort to entice Jake into a traveling adventure to South America to remedy some ill-understood notion that his (Cohn's) life was insufficiently "full." Frances is not one of Hemingway's appealing women: she is jealous, possessive, and manipulative. Although sufficiently liberated to pursue a career, Frances has grown desperate of late, eager to marry—to marry Cohn specifically, who, as Jake satirically observes, "never had a chance of not being taken in hand."

Jake is dismayed (and amused) by Cohn's romanticism—his belief that a way exists to "fix" his life by moving it to an exciting new place. Especially baffling to Jake is Cohn's reliance on books like *The Purple Land*. As suggested by its title, this novel about amorous adventures with happy endings, if taken by a man of thirty-four "as a guide-book to what life holds," is, according to Jake, "about as safe as it would be for a man of the same age to enter Wall Street direct from a French convent, equipped with a complete set of ... [Horatio] Alger books."

By contrast, Jake implies about himself that he is a man of few illusions. Here it is important to note that Jake—both protagonist and narrator—is telling the unfolding story from his own perspective. He works as a newspaper reporter but the reader must bear in mind that objectivity about personal matters is rarely achieved. By the end of these opening chapters Hemingway has created two distinct sensibilities. Jake and Cohn have in common being more productively engaged and forward-looking (less "lost") than their more dissolute companions. Cohn, however, lives with a certain "expectancy," an assumption that life can be better than it actually is, and Jake adopts the more sober awareness that there is no escaping the limitations of the self. In simplified terms, Cohn yearns, Jake accepts; Cohn is the romantic, Jake, the stoic.

Many commentators lament (and find unnecessary) the prominent anti-Semitism in the novel associated with Cohn, but it was a widespread and socially acceptable bigotry at that time. Cohn's "Jewishness" has little bearing on his fate in the novel. All sorts of people believe life in "purple lands" is possible and desirable; it is this error of judgment that is more importantly responsible for the suffering Cohn undergoes and inflicts.

The scene that opens Chapter III recurs at different sites throughout the novel and is likely the reason that Dutch critic Nico Rost dismissed Hemingway's characters as "the new Bohemians with checkbooks" (*Ernest Hemingway in Holland, 1925-1981,* ed., Bakker, p. 9). Here begin the much-discussed rhythms of bar- and café-hopping in which Hemingway's expatriate crowd seems permanently caught, perpetually seeking the social distractions a good city offers: noisy parties and crowds, food, and alcohol. On some familiar but unarticulated impulse, Jake picks up Georgette, the pretty prostitute with the bad teeth. Drink and dinner follow, but not sex. Georgette, herself afflicted with a disease of the trade, encounters Jake's sexual impotence which he names his own "sickness." Thus does Hemingway introduce his version of what critic Mark Spilka calls "[o]ne of the most persistent themes of the twenties ... the death of love in WW I" (Spilka, *Merrill Studies in "The Sun Also Rises."* ed, White, p.73). Prostitution is, of course, not a postwar novelty but it provides here a specific instance of the degradation of sex for money. Georgette's brief presence in this scene initiates a comparison of the women in the novel. Georgette, a streetwalker, is smart, plucky, and self-reliant; she knows how to get her money's worth and is socially savvy enough to form an immediate dislike for Frances and her domineering airs. Hemingway's play with irony is at work here too. Jake, an impotent man, jokes with his friends about being engaged to a "Georgette" with a different name, a famous singer and beautiful lesbian well-known to Parisians.

With the sudden appearance of Brett at the bar it is again important to remember that the Jake in the scene at its enactment in real time is not the same Jake who is reporting retrospectively. With Brett come pain and complexity in both versions of the scene. Jake's harmless enjoyment of Georgette's uncomplicated companionship can likely be repeated at a later time (one of his losses) but Brett's allure has been profoundly altered for him by the intervening action he has yet to relate. Of this scene, critic James Nagel writes:

> Brett appears, ironically for a woman of unusually active heterosexual appetite, with a group of male homosexuals.... At the time he first sees her, Jake is in the company of Georgette, a prostitute he picked up for dinner. Both of these lovers are with inappropriate companions, and they gravitate to each other with unstated assurance. Jake is offended by the effeminate manner of Brett's companions, and she jibes him about the restraint of trade that his date represents. From the beginning, the world is out of sexual order, the social evening a parody of erotic potential, and the deeper irony is that this pathology is at the very heart of Jake and Brett's relationship. Their conversation in the taxi reveals the central problem of the novel: that they love one another, that they feel there is nothing they can do about it, that it is painful and destructive for them to be together (24). Whatever else happens is driven by this fact, and it is impossible for them to change it. (Nagel, "Brett and the other women in *The Sun Also Rises*," *Cambridge Companion*, p.94.)

In this scene we encounter another prevailing bigotry of the times: disdain for homosexuality. Jake's anger at the gay men who arrive with Brett makes sense only as a defensive posture against his own deprivation. A common stereotype of the uncommon but newly emerging "new woman" is also introduced here. Brett Ashley is English but she is of the same age and times that brought suffrage to American women and the initial heady confidence that comes with feelings of liberation. Brett, the "new woman," smokes and drinks in public, drinks freely and often, appears in public with bare legs, associates with "unconventional" people, is overtly sexual while adopting the short hair and bold language traditionally linked with men. But she is also a fantasy figure and more than just "damned good-looking," as Jake and others observe about her more than once. In a remark that must have been influenced by the last page of *The Great Gatsby*, Hemingway has Jake describe Robert Cohn's "look of eager, deserving expectation" when he first looks at Brett: "He looked a great deal as his compatriot must have looked when he saw the promised land." From this early moment in the novel the sexual tension that permeates most of the interactions among members of Jake's crowd and that has so much to do with the outcome of the story begins to build. Cohn's doomed and incorrigibly romantic attraction to Brett is parallel to, but, in important ways, not similar to that of Jake for Brett.

Chapter IV provides the most explicit enactment of the doomed love between Jake and Brett. It moves swiftly from a rush of desire in the back seat of a dark taxi to anguished immobility: the two are left "sitting ... like two strangers" moments later—desire with no place to go. High-spirited Brett confesses to being "miserable" without Jake but "miserable" with him as well. To ward off her pain, she seeks out new company at a new bar as Jake retreats to his apartment on the Boulevard St. Michel. Here Hemingway allows the reader to see Jake by himself as he falls briefly into his own grief: the perverse war wound that has left him with sexual feeling but no sexual capacity—"You have given more than your life," the hospital colonel tells him—and the loss of Brett and the normal fulfillment of love that is its consequence. Of this feature of the novel, critic Michael S. Reynolds writes:

We know that Jake was a U. S. Navy pilot flying on the Italian front during the war where he was wounded in the

groin. We never see the wound, but we learn implicitly that Jake has all the sexual drives of a normal man but has none of the physical equipment to satisfy those drives. From this information, we must assume that his testicles are intact and his phallus is missing. Hospitalized in England, Jake falls in love with his nurse, Brett Ashley: the sexually incapable man and the sexually active woman—a punishment that might have come from Dante's *Inferno*.
(Reynolds, *The Sun Also Rises: A Novel of the Twenties*, p. 25).

Uncharacteristically, Jake weeps. Brett's drunken and amorous intrusion at this vulnerable moment and hour (4:30 A.M.) while the Count is waiting up the street only exacerbates Jake's pain. He falls asleep: "It is awfully easy to be hard-boiled about everything in the daytime, but at night it's another thing." Nagel comments:

> The central dilemma for Jake is whether he can change the situation by finding some satisfaction in life. The problem for Brett is that she needs the companionship of a man, and no one but Jake can offer her much beyond fleeting sexual pleasure (ibid. 94).

In **Chapter V** with Jake out early in the morning, he can be hard-boiled. More than that: he can enjoy his life. Critic Michael Reynolds observes:

> If the story is a sad one, if Jake does participate knowingly in his own disgrace, if the other characters have so few redeeming values, then why does *The Sun Also Rises* continue to intrigue readers? ....The answers ... reside in Hemingway's extraordinary ability to create the ambience of a special time and place. When Jake walks "down the Boulevard to the rue Soufflot for coffee and brioche" (35), we walk with him and agree that it is a fine morning.... Everyone wants to go to Paris. Jake's ambles along the boulevards serve to increase our appetite....
> (Reynolds, p. 44.)

Without the presence of Brett (or any woman), Jake re-enters the stream of humanity and enjoys it. Not at all aimless, he heads off to his office to work that he enjoys. (Of the major characters, only Jake and Pedro work to support themselves. Cohn writes but is mainly supported by Frances and his mother. Brett has alimony and will soon rely on her fiancé, Mike, who, in turn, intends to rely on his distant and wealthy family for support.) Jake's brief encounter with fellow correspondents Woolsey and Krum is Hemingway's moment to make an unsubtle jab at the tedium he saw befalling most married men: "You know how it is, though, with a wife and kids." In this relatively carefree chapter Hemingway puts a reminder of one "trap" Jake will escape. (Hemingway avoided this same perceived trap by acquiring four different wives.) The dialogue between Jake and Cohn at lunch about Brett and Cohn's attraction to her indirectly calls to mind the impermanence of romantic union and perfectly illustrates the differences between the two men. Cohn is idealistic, chivalric, confessional, and undefended; Jake is understated, detached, hidden, realistic, and cynical.

In **Chapter VI**, before being trapped in the wretched scene where Frances publicly heaps abuse on Cohn, Jake interestingly discloses that his own anger at Cohn for falling in love with Brett has made for a lukewarm appraisal of his romantic friend. He remedies this failing by acknowledging (not quite praising) Cohn's athleticism, manly attractiveness, and boyishly cheerful nature. This defense helpfully keeps the reader from dismissing Cohn as hopelessly pathetic in the next scene when Hemingway unleashes his considerable disdain for (what he perceives as) the possessive, manipulative woman. Which Frances, dreadfully in this scene, is. She is emasculating: "This one"—she speaks of Cohn to Jake in the third person—"didn't come home for lunch"; and sarcastic: "That was a fine girl you had at the dances, and then went off with that Brett one." Privately to Jake she unwittingly reveals herself to be a self-pitying, aging, and anxious woman. Jake wonders, "Why did [Cohn] sit there.... taking it like that?" before fleeing the scene.

Chapter VII closes Book I. Jake is anticipating the arrival of his friend Bill Gorton and their planned trip to Spain for trout-fishing in the Irati River and the festival in Pamplona. Before leaving Paris, Jake has two important encounters with Brett and Count Mippipopolous. The Count is an odd fellow. He has propositioned Brett, offering ten thousand dollars if she'll go away with him, but Brett, not a prostitute, declines. The Count's reaction to Brett's rejection contrasts with that which Cohn will presently display: "He [the Count] was damn nice about it," says Brett, and later he offers to take her and Jake to dinner knowing they are in love. What makes for this good-natured and generous amorality is what makes the Count important to the novel. Robert E. Fleming writes:

> It is possible that Count Mippipopolous is one of the early prototypes in Hemingway's fiction of the character type known variously as the "code hero" or the "tutor" [Philip Young's phrase], a type whose minor character flaws are outweighed by his strict observation of a code. (Fleming, *Critical Essays*, ed. James Nagel, 141; see also Fleming's note 2, 145.)

Brett tells Jake the Count is "one of us" and the Count, as if offering a definition of this category of special people, says, "You must get to know the values." All three are the walking war-wounded—Jake and the Count with his arrow scars, literally, and Brett through losses of love and an abusive marriage. Having lost the best, what are the possible attitudes? The Count is explicit: "I have lived very much that now I can enjoy everything so well." And he does: feasting, enjoying the most expensive champagnes and brandies, and enjoying watching others in love having fun without having to personally participate. "I am always in love," he sums up. The Count's appeal and wisdom emanate partly from their mysterious origins. Such a perspective does not likely spring from managing a string of sweet shops in America. It is not an inevitable outcome of serving in "seven wars and four revolutions," either. Besides being appealing, the Count is also an entirely believable human being, even if his title is possibly not.

Hemingway's reputation as a writer who disliked or misrepresented women has generated quantities of a new kind of criticism in the last quarter century. Feminist writers Debra A. Moddelmog and Mimi Reisel Gladstein do not dispute the stereotypical and condescending attitude Hemingway had for women, but both seek primarily to treat Hemingway in his own context and to offer new readings to familiar passages. In *Reading Desire: In Pursuit of Ernest Hemingway* (1999) Moddelmog discusses homosexual themes in *The Sun Also Rises*. About Brett she writes,

> ...Brett's alcoholism and inability to sustain a relationship might be indications not of nymphomania, with which critics have often charged her, but of a dissatisfaction with the strictures of the male-female relationship. Brett's announcement, for example, that she can drink safely among homosexual men (22) can be taken to mean she cannot control her own heterosexual desire, though it could also reveal underlying anxiety toward the heterosexual desire of men. (Moddelmog, p. 95)

She also cites in support of her theory work presented by Peter Messent in *New Readings of the American Novel* where he discusses "gender fluidity" in *The Sun Also Rises*: "Among other things," she notes of Messent, "he points to Georgette's sexual forwardness with Jake, Brett's pre-dawn visit to Jake's room after he retired there with a 'headache,' the count's bringing of roses to Jake, and Jake's crying" (note 13, p. 166). Gladstein focuses on Brett's persona as a blend of Hemingway's division of the female into erotic fantasy and destructive force. Her insights are helpful for understanding later sections of the novel.

The drama in Book II takes place mainly in Pamplona, but before arriving there, Jake's crowd briefly scatters. In Chapter VII, Brett—on a whim—disappears with Cohn on a tryst they conceal from Jake. Frances also disappears but no one knows to where. Brett returns to meet up with her amiably drunken fiancé, Mike. Jake's comment to Bill after watching Mike's barely-concealed lust for Brett—"Mike was pretty excited about his girl friend"—is evidence of his daytime strategy of "hardboiled detachment." Cohn returns in a swoon over Brett, but is—to everyone's astonishment—eager to join the group that will include her fiancé Mike when they all converge at the festival. It is not Jake's idea that his Paris companions follow him to Spain on his planned vacation with Bill, but he graciously allows it to happen. Their presence becomes an intrusion of sorts, and the ensuing clash of values Hemingway sets up and its consequences contribute to raising the novel's significance beyond that of a period piece.

Bill's arrival brings humor and playful companionship to Jake (and more anti-Semitism in Cohn's company and even some anti-Catholic feeling later). On the train to Bayonne, they have an amusing encounter with a family from Montana traveling in Europe for the first time. Amusing for several reasons: both husband and wife speak in predictable American clichés: "Travel while you're young"; "See America first!", and the wife righteously chides her husband for sneaking a beer with his buddies on a fishing trip he recalls from long ago. Jake and Bill also encounter on the train seven cars-full of Catholic Americans from Dayton, Ohio, making a pilgrimage to Biarritz and Lourdes. These are not random encounters. Hemingway is having fun making points here and establishing some serious concerns as well. Jake and Bill feel obstructed by the sheer numbers and special services that this caravan of well-organized religion claims for itself. The fishing trip and stay in the wilderness are also sacred—more authentically so for Hemingway—as his use of religious language and imagery in the upcoming scenes makes clear. These are parallel pilgrimages: different ways of seeking and experiencing God. Other concerns (fears) of Hemingway's—the collapse of romantic love in marriage and the oppressive domestic life—are conveyed in a single word, when the husband refers to his wife as "Mother." Curiously, their young son is silent.

It is one of Hemingway's strengths as a writer that he can present a moving and memorable portrait of a man who is denied the love of a woman side-by-side with vignettes that semi-humorously illustrate some reasons for escaping the company of women. Actually, Hemingway's love stories often end with the death of one of the characters. It is his heroes who endure their experiences and they are usually alone. It was also not in Hemingway's own experience to write about a love sustained over decades.

Another strength noted by critics is Hemingway's famous "ear," what Philip Young called, "...a trap that caught every mannerism of speech, that is responsible for the fact that [his] characters come so alive and distinct" (Young, *Ernest Hemingway: A Reconsideration*, p. 85). With the exception of some dated clichés in the dialogue (Jake's affectionate "You bum!" to Bill on the fishing trip; Bill's "So long, fella" to Jake as they part company after the festival), Hemingway's conversations would work in any contemporary book. Young continues, "...taken as a whole the book is superb.... Hemingway's wide-awake senses fully evoke an American's Paris, a vacationer's Spain" (86). Especially praised is Hemingway's gift for dialogue that (for one example) captures so effectively the tone of unsophisticated Americans traveling by train across Europe. Critic Conrad Aiken observed:

> If one feature of "The Sun Also Rises" demands separate discussion, it is Mr. Hemingway's use of dialogue. The dialogue is brilliant. If there is better dialogue being written today I do not know where to find it....it is alive with the rhythm and idioms, the pauses and suspensions and innuendoes and shorthands, of living speech. (Aiken, "Expatriates," *Merrill Studies*, p. 4)

Carlos Baker reminds the reader of the statement Hemingway made in the introduction to *Men at War* (1942): "A writer's job is to tell the truth" (p. xv). Baker follows with this high praise:

No other writer of our time has so fiercely asserted, so pugnaciously defended, or so consistently exemplified the writer's obligation to speak truly. His standard of truth-telling has been, moreover, so high and so rigorous that he has very rarely been willing to admit secondary evidence, whether literary evidence or evidence picked up from other sources than his own experience. "I only know what I have seen," is a statement which comes often to his lips and pen. What he has personally done, or what he knows unforgettably by having gone through one version of it, is what he is interested in telling about. (Baker, "The Way It Was," *Merrill Studies*, p. 26)

What Hemingway had personally done, and deeply enjoyed, is presented in **Chapters X–XII**: the experience of traveling across the countryside, enjoying spontaneous interactions with the locals, and fishing in remote rivers. Book One ended in a mood of tedium and depletion, with a sense that another round of bar-hopping would not yield anything new. In the interlude between Paris and Pamplona, Hemingway creates an oasis that exists outside linear time and the tensions of civilization. In doing so he joins the mainstream of American fiction beginning with the Pilgrims seeking refuge from English oppression through James Fenimore Cooper's tales of innocents in the wilderness, Hawthorne's Hester Prynne fleeing to the woods to escape the punitive "gossips," Huck Finn's "lighting out for the territory," Thoreau sojourning to Walden, and Melville's Ishmael returning to the sea "whenever [he felt] November in [his] soul."

The approach to the Irati River covers some of the most beautiful Spanish (Basque) countryside. Hemingway's reverence permeates every sentence. True to character, passive Cohn sleeps through the experience while Jake and Bill silently acknowledge the wonder of it to each other. Having to slow down for animals in the road—in this case, two sleeping donkeys—is familiar to any European traveler and a memorable image for those who aren't. A sense of easy co-existence and true harmony between the wild, the pastoral, and the agrarian village life builds with each turn of the road and new vista.

The simple good living and the generous good nature of the Basque peasants are evident in the stopover at the posada. "There was a low, dark room with saddles and harness, and hay-forks made of white wood, and clusters of grapes and long sausages hanging from the roof. It was cool and dusky...." One of the women serving drinks gives change back to Jake because she misunderstands that the extra money Jake offers is his tip for her.

Religious values, or, more accurately, religious yearnings, are again brought up when Jake enters the beautiful dark cathedral to pray. He prays for everyone who comes to mind before getting sleepy. The moment doesn't work; his mind wanders and he concludes with regret that he is "a rotten Catholic." "I ... wished I felt religious," Jake confesses to himself, "maybe I would next time...." Later, in Pamplona, Brett won't even go into the cathedral. Traditional religious pathways are closed to these people. One way to understand Hemingway's novel is as a search for what can bring religious experience alive or, failing that, what might be a sacred substitute for it, and, failing that, what way may still be found to live well and with meaning. Jake's famous comment that he makes later in the novel is relevant here: "Perhaps as you went along you did learn something. I did not care what it was all about. All I wanted to know was how to live in it."

A reminder that even on this pristine adventure not all is idyllic comes in the annoying and persistent presence of Cohn who, not understanding that he is not welcome on the fishing trip, tags along for the sake of meeting up later with Brett. Her transient attentions to him in San Sebastian he has grossly misunderstood. In an impulsive moment of quite undetached self-disclosure, Jake admits (with some shame) that he enjoys watching Cohn's nervousness about Brett's imminent arrival: "I was blind, unforgivingly jealous of what had happened to him. The fact that I took it as a matter of course did not alter that any. I certainly did hate him." Cohn's "little spell of superiority" about his tryst with Brett is especially irksome.

Jake's observation—"He [Cohn] was being confidential and it was giving him pleasure…" could only have been written by one who observed and overheard many conversations. At the last minute Cohn chooses not to go, preferring instead to stay back to prepare himself for Brett.

Jake and Bill are relieved, as should also be the reader: with Cohn around the flow of companionship ("brotherhood of man") would not be effortless, and reverence for Creation's great beech trees, deep waters, and colorful firm trout would be compromised. Also missing would be the entertaining repartee that Jake and Bill create and enjoy together. Flaws are difficult to find in the five days on the Irati River with the important exception that nature here is an all-male refuge. Within Hemingway's context, all goes well. We witness the hard work and discipline (planning, procuring the proper fishing and traveling permits, walking over rough ground) required just to get to "the good place"—preparation that parallels the devotion and ascetic rituals associated with traditional religious experience. In his review of the novel ("The Sportsman's Tragedy," *Critical Essays*, p.49) Edmund Wilson finds also a restorative "appetite for the physical world."

Mark Spilka observes that the pleasures of living with heightened senses—"the techniques of making coffee and pitching camp… [of] fishing and eating"—"become so valuable [that those experiencing them don't] want to rush them: they bring health, pleasure, beauty, and a sense of order which is sorely missing in…civilized experience; they were part of a healing process, a private and imaginative means of wiping out the damage…" (Spilka, "The Death of Love in *The Sun Also Rises*," *Merrill Studies*, pp. 78–79). Moreover, the language and imagery are explicitly religious. The mystery of origins comes out in Jake and Bill's joking about the old chicken and egg enigma. Most importantly, Bill possesses gratitude, the primary religious emotion: "Our stay on earth is not for long. Let us rejoice and believe and give thanks." "This is country," he says as they proceed through the silent woods, "Let no man be ashamed to kneel here in the great out-of-doors. Remember the woods were God's first temples." Bill's playful tone makes possible his deep respect.

One fact of life happily missing from the scene is tormented romantic love. Not only does Jake finally feel "good to be warm and in bed" but a soap opera-like tale Jake is reading about a bride willing to wait twenty-four years for the frozen body of her fiancé to emerge from a glacier and thaw is upstaged by Bill's arrival with his catch of beautiful fish. For which Jake feels appropriate reverence; he puts aside the book and forgets it. No unnecessary suffering is allowed: Jake bangs the fish against the dam so it dies instantly.

Humor is present also. Hemingway scholar Scott Donaldson devotes his chapter in *New Essays* (1987) to "Humor in *The Sun Also Rises.*" He finds Bill, bringer of high spirits, to be Hemingway's funniest character in this novel, beginning with his "stuffed dog" jokes. In the fishing interlude, Donaldson writes, "Bill makes fun of the clichés of literary criticism, Bible Belt morality, H. L. Mencken, and, especially, the Scopes trial and William Jennings Bryan's rhetoric in attacking the theory of evolution" (*New Essays*, p.36). He goes on:

… in the very subject matter of his humor, Hemingway conveys an attitude toward existence available to all…. The religious preach brotherhood and arrange for special privileges. The do-gooding…Prohibitionists [do] no good. The know-nothingism of what are currently called "creationists" is ridiculous, and so is the catchword pedantry of the literati: Irony and Pity. (pp 37–38)

Hemingway concludes his idyllic interlude: "There was no word from Robert Cohn nor from Brett and Mike." It is these characters who will, in the Pamplona section of Book II, contaminate the action and severely compromise Jake's experience of the festival. Although Jake participates in his own fall from grace, we see him first in **Chapter XIII** being greeted by Montoya, the hotel-keeper and promoter and protector of the most promising bullfighters. Jake has received Montoya's highest blessing; he is accepted as an *aficionado* which entitles him to be "one of us" in a second select community, this one even more rarified than that of the Count. Although uncommonly achieved or seen, the quality of *afición* is universal and available to all. It is an existential attitude: a willingness to live at the edge of life and death, an appreciation for the balance of art and skill and courage in the face of death. In Hemingway's story, it is manifested in its purist form by the best matador as he faces each bull and the risk of being fatally gored. Jake says, "Montoya could forgive anything of a bullfighter who had aficion…. At once he forgave me all of my friends." But this is before their wretched behavior and Brett's seduction of young Pedro Romero, most favored by Montoya, with Jake's shameful assistance. Thrown together now at the festival with no way out while it lasts, Jake's group finds that its competing personal agendas, the suppressed sexual tensions of their collective jealousies and rivalries, begin to escalate.

Before these tensions dominate the story, Hemingway offers the reader his reverent knowledge of the art of bullfighting. He is famous for the specificity he brings to descriptions of the performances in the bullring and the rituals that precede and follow them. Jake has Hemingway's experience here. He explains the use of the steers to "quiet" the bulls to keep them from breaking their horns against the walls or goring each other. The steer (castrated bulls) perform a service in the fiesta and are themselves often gored, sometimes fatally. "Must be swell being a steer," says Mike. Later in the café, discussion of the steer triggers the first ugly scene. Crudely and cruelly, Mike ridicules Cohn for publicly displaying his unwelcome and ill-founded ardor for Brett: "*Is* Robert Cohn going to follow Brett around like a steer all the time?" He jokes about Cohn's comparison of Brett with Circe, Homer's wily woman who turned men into swine, and scorns him for making literary allusions. Cohn's bad behavior rests on his "not getting it." Not cynical about life like the others (and with no personal experience of war), he has naïvely misread Brett's intentions at San Sebastian and now seems to be standing around passively waiting for life to turn out differently. When not imagining himself as Circe's victim, Cohn plays the knight to her maiden by insisting that it was his chivalry that successfully led Brett and Mike to this remote spot. Even Brett's "What rot!" fails to deflate him. The dialogue in these scenes is realistic enough to create discomfort and embarrassment for the reader. On the issue of reader discomfort, Michael Reynolds makes this more general comment: "If Frances Clyne makes the reader as uncomfortable as she makes Jake Barnes, if Brett Ashley leaves us a bit irritated with her random sexual encounters, perhaps this is how Hemingway wanted us to feel.... Perhaps he was telling his times as truly as he knew how: the usual supports that sustained the previous generation were no longer functioning properly" (Reynolds, 66–67).

Something, some social restraints and decency, is clearly missing from this important scene. Mike, never an impressive guy, was at least amiable in his first appearances. In these scenes he becomes considerably less likeable. Drink makes him careless and he is nearly always drunk, or "tight." Carelessness, or some absence of propriety, allows him to impulsively reveal his financial weaknesses. He went bankrupt in two ways: "Gradually and then suddenly." His abuse of money and flagrant mistreatment of his creditors follow him everywhere and later create a near brawl that reflects badly on the whole crowd. At Brett's urging (to entertain or undermine) he laughingly tells an unfunny story about himself and seems unaware of, or not to care about, the questions it raises about his character. With no thought for consequences, he one night gave away the war medals earned by another soldier to all the gushing girls at his table and laughed off the subsequent efforts others made to retrieve them. This callous denigration of military heroism is part of the cultural loss Hemingway is chronicling. The scene ends with a pleasant dinner at a café; pleasant because all the characters briefly pull together their best ("nice") selves. The others also dislike Cohn but disapprove of Mike's excesses. Jake is prescient. He writes that dinner reminds him of other dinners during the war: "There was much wine, an ignored tension, and a feeling of things coming that you cannot prevent happening." Pleasantly drunk, he can look at his friends and not feel "disgusted." His stoicism is at work here as well.

Jake's wakeful ruminations fill **Chapter XIV**. Waiting for the big celebrations to come, he has time to reflect again on his life, especially his relationship to Brett and other women. Providing some unity to the story is this second nighttime scene of Jake's vulnerability: "To hell with women, anyway. To hell with you, Brett Ashley." He reflects that Brett's loyalty to him has been a gift and then makes a fundamental observation about the condition of being human: you don't get something for nothing. "The bill always came," he comments, aware that Brett is with Mike in the hotel room next to his. In fact, Jake pays more of his share of life's little bills. He pays for the fishing permits, the reservations, for Georgette's ride home, for food and taxis and most of the bar tabs. But Jake is not defeated by this reality: "You paid some way for everything that was any good…. Either you paid by learning about them, or by experience, or by taking chances, or by money. Enjoying living was learning to get your money's worth and knowing when you had it…. The world was a good place to buy in." This reflection is one feature of Jake's philosophy for living. But in this time of keen disillusionment and cultural turmoil, insight is especially unreliable, or at least transient: "In five years … it will seem just as silly as all the other fine philosophies I've had." One of Jake's strengths that will later sustain him is evident here: he is willing and sufficiently courageous to live without certainty. An honest and reflective man, Jake surrenders himself—a genuine religious posture—to mystery and uncertainty: "I did not care what it was all about. All I wanted to know was how to live in it." Jake's maturity here is not enough to keep tormenting thoughts at bay. He thinks about Brett again, this time about her manner of speech, and returns to his reading, this time Turgenev, a better choice than melodramas about frozen fiancés.

In **Chapter XV** the festival "explodes." Peasants and tourists flood into the streets. At the sight of the fifers, drummers, and singers flowing past with banners reading "Hurray for Wine! Hurray for the Foreigners!" clueless Cohn asks, "Where are the foreigners?" Under the spell of the celebrations, Jake has the pleasant but dangerously false illusion that "nothing could have any consequences." When the *riau-riau* dancers chanting their magical mysteries surround Brett but don't permit her to join their dancing we are reminded again of her mesmerizing good looks and goddess-like capacity to inspire fantasy. We see another of Jake's appealing qualities here. A savvy and respectful traveler, he behaves with the peasants as few Americans would: he wants to buy a leather wine-skin and when they learn he wants it for its proper purpose and not as a tourist object to re-sell for profit somewhere else they happily offer it to him at the lowest price. Later a stranger insists on showing Jake how to properly break in his wine-skin. The natives trust him with their small rituals while Robert Cohn sleeps through them as earlier he slept through the beautiful countryside. It is consistent with what we know of Hemingway that he is suggesting here that Cohn is not quite "man enough" to "hold his liquor."

A reminder of the life-and-death stakes in the fiesta comes when a man falls during the running of the bulls and, it is later learned, dies. A reminder of the singular quality of the festival (and Jake's and Hemingway's familiarity with it) comes with Jake's mention of the peculiar humming sound: "The café did not make this same noise at any other time…. This hum went on, and we were in it and a part of it." A warning of the gruesome aspect of the ritual comes with the sight of the horses being gored. Earlier, Cohn had predicted, inexplicably, that he might be bored, but then finds himself bothered by their suffering. Hemingway would disapprove, but readers then and now may agree and find Cohn's compassion admirable. Predictably, Brett has a more traditionally male response; she can look at everything, even the bloodied horses, without flinching. Approvingly, Mike calls her an "extraordinary wench."

In this chapter we meet one of Hemingway's heroes and he is a mere boy: nineteen-year-old matador Pedro Romero. Romero is in control even outside the bullring. When Jake meets him he says, "You know English." Pedro smiles and says no. Like a rock star he has hangers-on, but does not appear to be arrogant or self-absorbed. In a remark similar to one

Jake made about Brett, he tells us that Romero was "the best-looking boy I have ever seen." In the bullring "Romero was the whole show." He is by far the best bullfighter, choosing not to make it easy for himself by unnecessarily exhausting his bull, choosing instead to work close to the horns of each one. In this way he demonstrates both courage and the subtle artistry of his skill, and makes of the action something more like ceremony and "less of a spectacle with unexplained horrors." "Romero's bull-fighting gave real emotion," Jake observes. Brett cannot keep her eyes off him and despite his age makes clear her attraction to him.

In **Chapter XVI** Jake's observation that the stormy weather fails to stop the fiesta but sends it "under cover" instead also describes the corruption about to occur—the contamination of the pious and happy festival brought on by a surrender to self-indulgence and all the self-centered emotions that such surrender brings to the surface in human relationships. Both fate (the war and Jake's wound) and human weaknesses are responsible for the sense of loss and the related rivalries and sexual tensions exhibited by the group. In this highly charged atmosphere, these tensions now lead inexorably to the violence and betrayal that spoil not just Jake's vacation, but, much more importantly, his valued friendship with Montoya and the group's collective experience. "Everybody behaves badly," Jake will later observe. "Give them the proper chance." Following Jake's disgraceful decision to arrange for the tryst between Brett and Romero—what Michael Reynolds calls the disturbing spectacle of a "sexually maimed war veteran [pimping] for a sexually rapacious woman" (50)—Montoya won't even nod to him. The trust has been broken. Brett has regret for causing Cohn's suffering although she vehemently states, "I hate his damned suffering." Inexplicably she uses her guilt about Cohn to justify her conquest of Romero. They hastily slip out the door together out of Montoya's sight. A code of honorable values and honest self-awareness seem unavailable to these characters.

In **Chapter XVII** Jake is dismayed to learn that Mike has had the effrontery to approach Montoya for a loan. This shameless gesture reveals Mike's utter lack of awareness of appropriate behavior or the nature of his indebtedness to Jake. He has encroached on a sacred trust and contributed to the final breakdown of that invaluable friendship. Also broken in this chapter is Jake's friendship with Cohn and whatever friendship Cohn had with the others. Cohn himself is broken. Drunken and bereft after seeing Brett walk out with Romero and ruin his own "affair with a lady of title," Cohn becomes, in Mark Spilka's words, "a knight-errant" who knocks down his rivals:

> With Jake and Mike he has no trouble, but when he charges into Pedro's room to rescue Brett, the results are disastrous: Brett tells him off, the bullfighter refuses to stay knocked down.... Cohn retires to his room, alone and friendless.... [T]he Romantic Hero has finally met his match. As the clash between them shows, there is a difference between physical and moral victory, between chivalric stubbornness and real self-respect. Thus Pedro fights to repair an affront to his dignity; though he is badly beaten, his spirit is untouched by his opponent, whereas Cohn's spirit is completely smashed.... Cohn has based his manhood on skill at boxing, or upon a woman's love, never upon internal strength; but now, when neither skill nor love supports him, he has bludgeoned his way to his own emptiness. (Spilka, *Merrill Studies*, p. 81)

At Bill's urging Jake reluctantly goes to Cohn's room where he finds him on his bed crying. Jake notes that Cohn is wearing a white polo shirt of the kind he'd worn at Princeton. Moments earlier Jake has himself been drawn back to a memory from his adolescent football-playing days. The polo shirt perhaps reminds Jake of Cohn's boxing days at Princeton where even when winning he felt himself an outsider. Here in full humiliation and defeat, Cohn speaks about suffering, but only his own. Jake is restrained; he knows this is not his scene. His suffering is done in private. Graciously and generously he assents when Cohn asks for forgiveness. Cohn states that he will leave the next day but does not say to where or if he intends ever to re-connect with any of the group.

If Mike could behave in a more unseemly manner he does so in **Chapter XVIII**. But the chapter belongs to Pedro Romero. Bruised but not humiliated, Romero performs to the highest standards of the sport and kills several bulls including the most magnificent and dangerous. All in attendance enthusiastically offer him their highest acclaim.

Commenting on the central significance Hemingway gave to bullfighting in his life and fiction, critic Mark Shorer recalls a revealing author's note Hemingway made in *Scribner's Magazine*: "I've known some very wonderful people who even though they were going directly to the grave ... managed to put up a fine performance enroute." A fine performance may be what remains for those who have lost all connection with the values that sustained previous generations. Those characters in the novel, Shorer writes:

> ... without belief, without relation to a cultural or national past, without ideological relation to the future ... submerge themselves in extravagant sensation and view life as a losing game, a sport like bullfighting which, while it is more nearly tragedy than sport because death is inevitable, is interesting only if it observes strict rules.... The preoccupation with bullfighting is not accidental; bullfighting is at once the most violent and stylized of sports. Its excitement depends on the degree to which the matador exposes himself to death *within the rules*. It disregards consequences, regards performance. Both are important. Courage, or unconcern for disaster, is a moral virtue: the best bullfighter works closest to the horns: the best man disregards present and impending catastrophe. (Shorer, "The Background of a Style," *Kenyon Review* 3, No. 1 [Winter 1941]: 101–3)

These insights amplify Jake's much-quoted comment: "All I wanted to know was how to live in it." The *how* is the performance. Some Hemingway readers will find that a value system embedded in performance alone is insufficient to sustain a person or a civilization. It is difficult, for example, to imagine Brett Ashley aging. Mike Campbell seems doomed to become a mainly harmless drunk, but Brett has more awareness than Mike and she has loyally sustained a love, however frustrated, for Jake. Will impulsive trysts and sexual sensation mean as much when she is fifty? Will the small delights of Paris street life and fishing trips with good companions still satisfy? These are not rhetorical questions but neither do they have satisfactory answers for many thoughtful readers. Hemingway himself expressed dismay at the destruction for commercial purposes of a beloved landscape he had chosen to re-visit. Critic Delmore Schwartz has a different perspective. He writes:

> The desire for sensation is not the sensuality of the dilettante, but a striving for genuine individuality. The sensations of the immediate present have an authenticity which the senses make self-evident. Above all, those sensations which occur in the face of grave danger reveal the self's essential reality, since in the face of extreme threat, the self must depend wholly upon its own skill, strength, and courage. Thus it is literally true that Hemingway's preoccupation with sensation is a preoccupation with genuine selfhood, moral character, and conduct.... Any concern with the self and its moral character requires a moral code, and the moral code in Hemingway is unmistakable. The rules of the code require honesty, sincerity, self-control, skill, and above all, personal courage. (Swartz, "The Fiction of Ernest Hemingway," *Perspectives USA*, Intercultural Publications, 1955, pp. 258–259)

After the debacle with Cohn and the closing of the festival there is a final gathering of the crowd before they head out in their separate directions. The conversation is tired and there is a silent acknowledgement of depletion and loss. Cohn is too humiliated to appear and has no doubt already left. Brett is off to Madrid with Romero. The loss is real. Jake comments, "The three of us sat at the table, and it seemed as though about six people were missing."

Book III, although brief, contains much that is predictable about the main characters and some that is not. Hemingway is not a writer who tells his reader what to think or expect. He has given us vividly imaginable scenes, sharp dialogue, and the characters in action. At the end it is impossible to know with any certainty what will become of any of these people. Mike has headed off with the hope that he'll find some place where his credit is still good. Jake and Bill have parted with a convincing exchange of mutual affection despite the clichés of speech. They will see each other again. Jake decides to spend his second week of vacation on the beaches of San Sebastian. Before leaving he makes a rare and discreet gesture of deep feeling: he rubs the rod-case of his fishing gear through the dust so that he will carry with him some connection to Spain and the fiesta.

Along the way Jake continues with his habit of interacting with the locals; he comes up with some semi-humorous observations about the differences between France and Spain that likely are a reflection of Hemingway's preference for the old-world traditions and people of Spain. In San Sebastian Jake takes a room and writes his now-confessional story as if he were a detached reporter of his own life. Jake has always been reflective and aware and concerned for honesty. He has just experienced a loss of beloved and well-earned achievement and he has lost Brett in a way different from the past. Although he does not reveal the depth of feeling he carries with these new losses, he makes it evident in the minute attention he gives to the details of his setting and activity, as if he needs to gather it into one safe and reliable whole. We see the piles of laundry, the books carefully placed near the bedside, his shaving materials laid out. We can feel the re-invigoration that comes from plunging into the depths of the ocean. Jake has returned himself to the enjoyment of what is there to be enjoyed. He can settle for wine as good company and not feel bitter. He can be amused by the biker's boils. He can sleep. When Brett's telegram comes summoning him to the rescue, Jake, before leaving, has this moment of self-awareness: "That was it. Send a girl off with one man. Introduce her to another to go off with him. Now go and bring her back. And sign the wire with love. That was it all right. I went into lunch." Readers differ on Jake's tone—resignation, bitterness, bemusement, relief—all are possible. Hemingway gives no clues. On the train to Madrid, Jake once again cannot sleep. He notes without comment that the station he is heading to in Madrid is at the "end of the line. All trains finish there. They don't go on anywhere." Three references to a dead end is perhaps a clue.

Jake finds Brett small and trembling in the hotel room she has shared with Romero. She is once again "miserable." She explains that she sent Romero away because she had decided not "to be one of these bitches that ruins children." When she states that she is acting here for Romero's own good the reader may remember that earlier she gave the same explanation to Jake for seducing Cohn into going to San Sebastian; it was also "for his own good." Overcome now with emotion and exhaustion, Brett weeps and vows not ever to speak of the affair again. Moments later in the bar she brings him up again, disclosing to Jake that she was not Romero's first woman. She appears to have some genuine concern that she may have hurt his career and his innocence, but concludes that she has not, that she ended things in time. "You know it makes one feel rather good deciding not to be a bitch," she says. "It's sort of what we have instead of God." At the festival Jake discourages Brett from going into a church because she won't understand the language. Much more is suggested here. Jake is a "rotten Catholic" but he has the values. For reasons suggested by Mike's comments to the group in Pamplona about Brett's own losses and her abusive and loveless marriage ("She hasn't had an absolutely happy life, Brett. Damned shame, too. She enjoys things so"), Brett has lost all possibility of ever feeling at home in church. After the scene at the church she goes to get her fortune told by a group of Gypsies.

Brett has been variously interpreted as a nymphomaniac and Circe-like destroyer of men. Robert W. Lewis likens Brett to the woman in Ecclesiastes whose "heart is snares and nets"

(Lewis, *Hemingway on Love*, p.34). These observations are not disputable but other readers are more sympathetic. Mimi Reisel Gladstein calls Brett one of the "destructive indestructibles" but asserts that this quality is not always her fault because, for one thing, she is devastatingly attractive to men (Gladstein, *The Indestructible Women in Faulkner, Hemingway, and Steinbeck*, p. 59). Gladstein puts some of the blame on the men for allowing their attraction to become worshipful. "The men in her life serve her in much the same manner as religious prostitutes served Aphrodite. First they worship at her shrine; then they prostitute themselves" (60).

At Pamplona Brett explains her pursuit of Romero as a way to break out of a pattern. Whatever way the reader may wish to understand Brett's reasoning here it is clear that she cares about being a respectful and respectable person. Critic Linda Patterson Miller bases her assessment on this aspect of Brett's perspective. Brett, she says, comes to realize that "Romero loved her and not the idea of her: 'He thinks it was me,' Brett repeats emphatically. 'Not the show in general' " (Miller, "Brett Ashley: The Beauty of It All," *Critical Essays*, p. 181). Patterson continues:

> Although Brett is visibly shaken when Jake arrives at the hotel in Madrid... she has discovered a new sense of self. She has come to realize what Jake tried to tell Cohn at the beginning of the novel, that 'you won't get away from yourself by moving from one place to the other.'... Brett is the one who has the potential for the clearest vision, and the emphasis upon her eyes, her 'watching' and 'seeing,' endorses her final recognition that she has herself.... In the themes of appearance and reality, and of personal growth and self-realization, *The Sun Also Rises* is very much her novel, and she stands at the center of it, beautiful, vulnerable, and finally herself. (182)

Concluding interpretations of Jake are nearly as various. In some ways Jake has been as much a fool for love as Cohn; he has compromised his *aficion* to give Brett what she wants.

But the telling observation about him, his saving grace, is that unlike the others in his circle of friends, he suffers in silence. Watching Brett and all her antics with men he holds his losses closely to himself, including the wound that makes impossible the overcoming of radical aloneness, the unalterable condition of being human. Critic Philip Young is the critic best known for the emphasis he puts on Hemingway's own experience of being wounded and the meaning the wound has in his novels. Young quotes a passage from Hemingway's story, "A Natural History of the Dead," in which an attending doctor instructs his aide to "hold tight" to the screaming wounded lieutenant: "He is in much pain. Hold him very tight." Young goes on, "As doctors are not always available, and are often of little use, holding tight against pain is an exercise ... important to the Hemingway hero ... the effort to hold tight developed into what is known as the Hemingway 'code'" (Young, "The Hero and the Code," *Ernest Hemingway: A Reconsideration*, p.56).

Earl Rovit makes the same point differently:

> Jake's impotency ... forces him to be a spectator rather than participator in the events of the novel. He can react intensely, but his actions will necessarily be passive; they will be struggles to "hold on" and to accept rather than to shape circumstances by force of his direct will. Thus the novel is composed largely of "what happens" to Jake and how he copes with these happenings over which he is denied any control.... [T]his places him in a constant psychological situation of having to accept the absurd meaninglessness of his fate and somehow wrest some meaning from it. (Rovit, pp 148–149)

Nearly all readers judge that what meaning Hemingway intends is contained in the last of the several taxi scenes. On their way to "see Madrid" the motion of the taxi brings Jake and Brett once again pressed against each other. Creating three separate instances of intimate activity in taxis is perhaps one way for Hemingway to achieve a sense of unity in the novel. In this scene are spoken the novel's famous last words:

> "Oh, Jake," Brett said, "we could have had such a damned good time together."
> Ahead was a mounted policeman in khaki directing traffic.
> He raised his baton. The car slowed suddenly pressing Brett against me.
> "Yes." I said. "Isn't it pretty to think so?"

We know that long-suffering Jake uses "pretty" ironically, but we do not know if irony will be the only or final perspective. Is their doomed love the consequence of official power as represented by the policeman with the raised baton? Does Jake realize that even were he not impotent Brett and he would not endure? Is human love itself doomed? Hemingway is noted for creating scenes so concretely and believably that the reader feels included in them.

James Nagel reminds the reader that *The Sun Also Rises* is "much more a novel of character than of event" (*Cambridge Companion*, p.90) and also that it is essentially confessional in nature:

> Jake has lost much during the summer of 1925, more than any other person in the book, and the very telling of the novel seems to be a confessional, an attempt to come to terms with what has happened, how his relationships have changed, what remains to give him the strength to get on with his life. His friendship with Robert Cohn has been destroyed; he has compromised his standing with the aficionados of Pamplona, and it would seem unlikely that he can go back for another fiesta, at least not to the hotel run by Montoya; and, most important, his love and respect for Brett have been tarnished. In short, Jake is not the same person after the festival that he was before. If it must be said that he had already lost more than he

deserved in World War I, he loses still more during the celebration in Spain, for much of what has sustained him is gone.

He is certainly one of the most isolated and vulnerable figures in American literature, and he narrates out of his disillusionment and pain, his grief evident throughout. As he says about himself, all he wants is to figure out how he can live in the world. It would seem that telling what happened is part of the process of learning how to live in the special circumstances of his world. (Nagel, "Brett and the Other Women in "*The Sun Also Rises*," *Cambridge Companion*, p. 90)

Jake has let go of certainty or even the hope of understanding very much about life. But as every reader recalls he cares about "how to live in it." Bill and Pedro Romero have found possible ways. Bill has the virtues of gratitude and honesty and the saving capacity for self-deprecating humor. Unlike Mike, Bill has humor that works without demeaning anyone. Only ideas and institutions are ridiculed. Romero has astonishing and admirable skills, but these work in a rarified world, not accessible to most people. Jake himself is the character many readers care most about. His way of living, carved out of his own fate and character, is generous and certainly the most authentic of all the novel's characters. What Hemingway appears to care about for his people is that wherever they find themselves, they live with authenticity in a world frequently hostile to the attainment of authenticity.

Critical Views

THE NEW YORK TIMES BOOK REVIEW OF
THE SUN ALSO RISES (1926)

Ernest Hemingway's first novel, "The Sun Also Rises," treats of certain of those younger Americans concerning whom Gertrude Stein has remarked: "You are all a lost generation." This is the novel for which a keen appetite was stimulated by Mr. Hemingway's exciting volume of short stories, "In Our Time." The clear objectivity and the sustained intensity of the stories, and their concentration upon action in the present moment, seemed to point to a failure to project a novel in terms of the same method, yet a resort to any other method would have let down the reader's expectations. It is a relief to find that "The Sun Also Rises" maintains the same heightened, intimate tangibility as the shorter narratives and does it in the same kind of weighted, quickening prose.

Mr. Hemingway has chosen a segment of life which might easily have become "a spectacle with unexplained horrors," and disciplined it to a design which gives full value to its Dionysian, all but uncapturable, elements. On the face of it, he has simply gathered, almost at random, a group of American and British expatriates from Paris, conducted them on a fishing expedition, and exhibited them against the background of a wild Spanish fiesta and bullfight. The characters are concisely indicated. Much of their inherent natures are left to be betrayed by their own speech, by their apparently aimless conversation among themselves. Mr. Hemingway writes a most admirable dialogue. It has the terse vigor of Ring Lardner at his best. It suggests the double meanings of Ford Madox Ford's records of talk. Mr. Hemingway makes his characters say one thing, convey still another, and when a whole passage of talk has been given, the reader finds himself the richer by a totally unexpected mood, a mood often enough of outrageous familiarity with obscure heartbreaks.

The story is told in the first person, as if by one Jake Barnes, an American newspaper correspondent in Paris. This approach notoriously invites digression and clumsiness. The way Mr. Hemingway plays this hard-boiled Jake is comparable to Jake's own evocations of the technique of the expert matador handling his bull. In fact, the bullfight within the story bears two relations to the narrative proper. It not only serves to bring the situation to a crisis, but it also suggests the design which Mr. Hemingway is following. He keeps goading Jake, leading him on, involving him in difficulties, averting serious tragedy for him, just as the matador conducts the bull through the elaborate pattern of danger.

The love affair of Jake and the lovely, impulsive Lady Ashley might easily have descended into bathos. It is an erotic attraction which is destined from the start to be frustrated. Mr. Hemingway has such a sure hold on his values that he makes an absorbing, beautifully and tenderly absurd, heartbreaking narrative of it. Jake was wounded in the war in a manner that won for him a grandiose speech from the Italian General. Certainly Jake is led to consider his life worse than death. When he and Brett (Lady Ashley) fall in love, and know, with that complete absence of reticences of the war generation, that nothing can be done about it, the thing might well have ended there. Mr. Hemingway shows uncanny skill in prolonging it and delivering it of all its implications.

No amount of analysis can convey the quality of "The Sun Also Rises." It is a truly gripping story, told in a lean, hard, athletic narrative prose that puts more literary English to shame. Mr. Hemingway knows how not only to make words be specific but how to arrange a collection of words which shall betray a great deal more than is to be found in the individual parts. It is magnificent writing, filled with that organic action which gives a compelling picture of character. This novel is unquestionably one of the events of an unusually rich year in literature.

Carlos Baker on Hemingway's skill at telling it "the way it was"

"A writer's job is to tell the truth," said Hemingway in 1942.[2] He had believed it for twenty years and he would continue to believe it as long as he lived. No other writer of our time has so fiercely asserted, so pugnaciously defended, or so consistently exemplified the writer's obligation to speak truly. His standard of truth-telling has been, moreover, so high and so rigorous that he has very rarely been willing to admit secondary evidence, whether literary evidence or evidence picked up from other sources than his own experience. "I only know what I have seen," is a statement which comes often to his lips and pen. What he has personally done, or what he knows unforgettably by having gone through one version of it, is what he is interested in telling about. This is not to say that he has refused to invent freely. But he has always made it a sacrosanct point to invert in terms of what he actually knows from having been there.

The primary intent of his writing, from first to last, has been to seize and project for the reader what he has often called "the way it was." This is a characteristically simple phrase for a concept of extraordinary complexity, and Hemingway's conception of its meaning has subtly changed several times in the course of his career—always in the direction of greater complexity. At the core of the concept, however, one can invariably discern the operation of three aesthetic instruments: the sense of place, the sense of fact, and the sense of scene.

The first of these, which is clearly a passion with Hemingway, is the sense of place. "Unless you have geography, background," he once told George Antheil, "you have nothing."[3] You have, that is to say, a dramatic vacuum. Few writers have been more place-conscious. Few have so carefully charted out the geographical groundwork of their novels while managing to keep background so conspicuously unobtrusive. Few, accordingly, have been able to record more economically and graphically the way it is when you walk through the streets of Paris in search of breakfast at a corner café. Or when your footfalls echo among surrounding walls on the ancient cobblestones of early morning Venice, heading for the market-place beside the Adriatic. Or when, at around six o'clock of a Spanish dawn, you watch the bulls running from the corrals at the Puerta Rochapea through the streets of Pamplona towards the bullring.

(...)

Along with the sense of place, and as a part of it, is the sense of fact. Facts march through all his pages in a stream as continuous as the refugee wagons in Thrace or the military camions on the road from the Isonzo. Speculation, whether by the author or by the characters, is ordinarily kept to a minimum. But facts, visible or audible or tangible facts, facts baldly stated, facts without verbal paraphernalia to inhibit their striking power, are the stuff of Hemingway's prose.

Sometimes, especially in the early work, the facts seem too many for the effect apparently intended, though even here the reader should be on guard against misconstruing the intention of a given passage. It is hard to discover, nevertheless, what purpose beyond the establishment of the sense of place is served by Barnes's complete itinerary of his walk with Bill Gorton through the streets of Paris.[6] The direction is from Madame Lecomte's restaurant on the Ile St. Louis across to the left bank of the Seine, and eventually up the Boulevard du Port Royal to the Café Select. The walk fills only two pages. Yet it seems much longer and does not further the action appreciably except to provide Jake and Bill with healthy after-dinner exercise. At Madame Lecomte's (the facts again), they have eaten "a roast chicken, new green beans, mashed potatoes, a salad, and some apple pie and cheese." To the native Parisian, or a foreigner who knows the city, the pleasure in the after-dinner itinerary would consist in the happy shock of recognition. For others, the inclusion of so many of the facts of municipal or gastronomic geography—so many more than are justified by their dramatic purpose—may seem excessive.

Still, this is the way it was that time in Paris. Here lay the bridges and the streets, the squares and the cafés. If you followed them in the prescribed order, you came to the café where Lady Brett Ashley sat on a high stool at the bar, her crossed legs stockingless, her eyes crinkling at the corners.

If an imaginative fusion of the sense of place and the sense of fact is to occur, and if, out of the fusing process, dramatic life is to arise, a third element is required. This may be called the sense of scene. Places are less than geography, facts lie inert and uncoordinated, unless the imagination runs through them like a vitalizing current and the total picture moves and quickens. How was it, for example, that second day of the San Fermin fiesta in the Pamplona bullring after Romero had killed the first bull?

"They had hitched the mules to the dead bull and then the whips cracked, the men ran, and the mules, straining forward, their legs pushing, broke into a gallop, and the bull, one horn up, his head on its side, swept a swath smoothly across the sand and out the red gate."[7]

Here are a dead bull, men, mules, whips, sand, and a red gate like a closing curtain—the place and the facts. But here also, in this remarkably graphic sentence, are the seven verbs, the two adverbs, and the five adverbial phrases which fuse and coordinate the diverse facts of place and thing and set them in rapid motion. If one feels that the sentence is very satisfying as a scene, and wishes to know why, the answer might well lie where it so often lies in a successful lyric poem—that is, in our sense of difficulty overcome. Between the inertness of the dead bull when he is merely *hitched* (a placid verb) and the smooth speed with which the body finally *sweeps* across the sand and out of sight, come the verbs of sweating effort: *crack, run, strain*, and *break*. It is precisely at the verb *broke*, that the sentence stops straining and moves into the smooth glide of its close. The massing, in that section of the sentence, of a half-dozen s's, compounded with the *th* sounds of *swath* and *smoothly*, can hardly have been inadvertent. They ease (or grease) the path of the bull's departure.

Notes
2. *Men at War* (New York, 1942), introduction, p. xv.
3. George Antheil, *Bad Boy of Music*, p. 278.
6. *SAR*, pp. 79–50.
7. *SAR*, p. 175.

MARK SPILKA ON THE RUINATION OF
"THE GOOD PLACE"

We must understand here that the war, the early football game, and the fight with Cohn have this in common: they all involve ugly, senseless, or impersonal forms of violence, in which a man has little chance to set the terms of his own integrity. Hence for Hemingway they represent the kinds of degradation which can occur at any point in modern society—and the violence at Pamplona is our current sample of such degradation. Indeed, the whole confluence of events now points to the social meaning of Jake's wound, for just as Cohn has reduced him to a dazed adolescent, so has Brett reduced him to a slavish pimp. When she asks for his help in her affair with Pedro, Barnes has no integrity to rely on; he can only serve her as Cohn has served her, like a sick romantic steer. Thus, for love's sake, he will allow her to use him as a go-between, to disgrace him with his friend Montoya, to corrupt Romero, and so strip the whole fiesta of significance. In the next book he will even run to her rescue in Madrid, though by then he can at least recognize his folly and supply his own indictment: "That was it. Send a girl off with one man. Introduce her to another to go off with him. Now go and bring her back. And sign the wire with love. That was it all right." It seems plain, then, that Cohn and Brett have given us a peacetime demonstration, postwar style, of the meaning of Jake's shell wound.

At Pamplona the demonstration continues. Brett strolls through the fiesta with her head high, "as though [it] were being staged in her honor, and she found it pleasant and amusing." When Romero presents her with a bull's ear "cut by popular acclamation," she carries it off to her hotel, stuffs it far back in the drawer of the bed table, and forgets about it. The ear was taken, however, from the same bull which had killed one of the crowd a few days before, during the dangerous bull-run through the streets; later the entire town attended the man's funeral, along with drinking and dancing societies from nearby communities. For the crowd, the death of this bull was a communal triumph and his ear a token of communal strength; for Brett the ear is a private trophy. In effect, she has robbed the community of its triumph, as she will now rob it of its hero. As an *aficionado*, Barnes understands this threat too well. These are decadent times in the bull ring, marred by false esthetics; Romero alone has "the old thing," the old "purity of line through the maximum of exposure": his corruption by Brett will complete the decadence. But mainly the young fighter means something more personal to Barnes. In the bull ring he combines grace, control, and sincerity with manliness; in the fight with Cohn he proves his integrity where skill is lacking. His values are exactly those of the hunter in "Francis Macomber," or of the fisherman in *The Old Man and the Sea*. As one of these few remaining images of independent manhood, he offers Barnes the comfort of vicarious redemption. Brett seems to smash this as she leaves with Pedro for Madrid. To ward off depression, Barnes can only get drunk and retire to bed; the fiesta goes on outside, but it means nothing now: the "good place" has been ruined.

As Book III begins, Barnes tries to reclaim his dignity and to cleanse himself of the damage at Pamplona. He goes to San Sebastian and sits quietly there in a café, listening to band concerts; or he goes swimming there alone, diving deep in the green waters. Then a telegram from Brett arrives, calling him to Madrid to help her out of trouble. At once he is like Cohn again, ready to serve his lady at the expense of self-respect. Yet in Madrid he learns to accept, emotionally, what he has always faintly understood. As he listens to Brett, he begins to drink heavily, as if her story has driven home a painful lesson. Brett herself feels "rather good" about sending Pedro away: she has at least been able to avoid being "one of these bitches that ruins children." This is a moral triumph for her, as Barnes agrees; but he can scarcely ignore its implications for himself. For when Brett refuses to let her hair grow long for Pedro, it means that her role in life is fixed: she can no longer reclaim her lost womanhood; she can no longer live with a fine man without destroying him. This seems to kill the illusion which is behind Jake's suffering throughout the novel: namely, that if he hadn't been wounded, if he had somehow survived the war with his manhood intact, then he and Brett would have become true lovers. The closing lines confirm his total disillusionment:

> "Oh, Jake," Brett said, "we could have had such a damned good time together."
>
> Ahead was a mounted policeman in khaki directing traffic. He raised his baton. The car slowed suddenly pressing Brett against me.
>
> "Yes," I said. "Isn't it pretty to think so?"

"Pretty" is a romantic word which means here "foolish to consider what could *never* have happened," and not "what can't happen now." The signal for this interpretation comes from the policeman who directs *traffic* between Brett's speech and Barnes's reply. With his khaki clothes and his preventive baton, he stands for the war and the society which made it, for the force which stops the lovers' car, and which robs them of their normal sexual roles. As Barnes now sees, love itself is dead for their generation. Even without his wound, he would still be unmanly, and Brett unable to let her hair grow long.

Yet, according to the opening epigraphs, if one generation is lost and another comes, the earth abides forever; and according to Hemingway himself, the abiding earth is the novel's hero. Perhaps he is wrong on this point, or at least misleading. There are no joyous hymns to the seasons in this novel, no celebrations of fertility and change. The scenic descriptions are accurate enough, but rather flat; there is no deep feeling in them, only fondness, for the author takes less delight in nature than in outdoor sports. He is more concerned, that is, with baiting hooks and catching trout than with the Irati River and more pleased with the grace and skill of the bullfighter than with the bull's magnificence. In fact, it is the bullfighter who seems to abide in the novel, for surely the bulls are dead like the trout before them, having fulfilled their roles as beloved opponents. But Romero is very much alive as the novel ends. When he leaves the hotel in Madrid, he "pays the bill" for his affair with Brett, which means that he has earned all its benefits. He also dominates the final conversation between the lovers, and so dominates the closing section. We learn here that his sexual initiation has been completed and his independence assured. From now on, he can work out his life alone, moving again and again through his passes in the ring, gaining strength, order, and purpose as he meets his own conditions. He provides no literal prescription to follow here, no call to bullfighting as the answer to Barnes's problems; but he does provide an image of integrity, against which Barnes and his generation are weighed and found wanting. In this sense, Pedro is the real hero of the parable, the final moral touchstone, the man whose code gives meaning to a world where love and religion are defunct, where the proofs of manhood are difficult and scarce, and where every man must learn to define his own moral conditions and then live up to them.

PHILIP YOUNG ON THE NOVEL AS HEMINGWAY'S WASTE LAND

At Pamplona the tension which all try to ignore builds up, slowly, and breaks finally as the events come to their climax simultaneously with the fiesta's. Then, in an intensely muted coda, a solitary Jake, rehabilitating himself, washes away his hangovers in the ocean. Soon it is all gone, he is returned to Brett as before, and we discover that we have come full circle, like all the rivers, the winds, and the sun, to the place where we began.

This is motion which goes no place. Constant activity has brought us along with such pleasant, gentle insistence that not until the end do we realize that we have not been taken in, exactly, but taken nowhere; and that, finally, is the point.[1] This is structure as meaning, organization as content. And, as the enormous effect the book had on its generation proved, such a meaning or content was important to 1926. The book touched with delicate accuracy on something big, on things other people were feeling, but too dimly for articulation. Hemingway had deeply felt and understood what was in the wind. Like Brett, who was the kind of woman who sets styles, the book itself was profoundly creative, and had the kind of power that is prototypal.

Despite quite a lot of fun *The Sun Also Rises* is still Hemingway's *Waste Land*, and Jake is Hemingway's Fisher King. This may be just coincidence, though the novelist had read the poem, but once again here is protagonist gone impotent, and his land gone sterile. Eliot's London is Hemingway's Paris, where spiritual life in general, and Jake's sexual life in particular, are alike impoverished. Prayer breaks down and fails, a knowledge of traditional distinctions between good and evil is largely lost, copulation is morally neutral and, cut off from the past chiefly by the spiritual disaster of the war, life has become mostly meaningless. "What shall we do?" is the same constant question, to which the answer must be, again, "Nothing." To hide it, instead of playing chess one drinks, mechanically and always. Love is a possibility only for the two who cannot love; once again homosexuality intensifies this atmosphere of sterility; once more the Fisher King is also a man who fishes. And again the author plays with quotations from the great of the past, as when in reply to Jake's remark that he is a taxidermist Bill objects, "That was in another country. And besides all the animals were dead."

To be sure, the liquor is good, and so are the food and the conversation. But in one way Hemingway's book is even more desperate than Eliot's. The lesson of an "asceticism" to control the aimless expression of lust would be to Jake Barnes only one more bad joke, and the fragments he has shored against his ruins are few, and quite inadequate. In the poem a message of salvation comes out of the life-giving rain which falls on western civilization. In Hemingway's waste land there is fun but no hope. No rain falls on Europe this time, and when it does fall in *A Farewell to Arms* it brings not life but death.

Notes

1. It happens that this is not precisely the point Hemingway intended to make. He once said that he regarded his first epigraph, "you are all a lost generation," as a piece of "splendid bombast." (Later he devoted one of the sketches, "Une Génération Perdue," of his *Moveable Feast* to an effective attack on the phrase.) It was his idea that the second epigraph taken from *Ecclesiastes* would "correct" the famous remark attributed to Miss Stein. As far as he was concerned, he wrote his editor Maxwell Perkins, the point of his novel is, as the Biblical lines say in part, that "the earth abideth forever."

Some support for this position can be found in the novel itself. Not quite all the people in it are "lost"—surely Romero is not—and the beauty of the eternal earth is now and then richly evoked. But most of the characters do seem a great deal of the time if not lost then terribly unsure of their bearings, and few readers have felt the force of Hemingway's intention. The strongest feeling in the book is that for the people in it (and one gets the distinct impression that other people do not matter very much) life is futile, and their motions like the motion of the sun of the title (as it appears to our eyes): endless, circular, and unavailing. Further, for all who remember what the Preacher said in this well-known Biblical passage, the echo of "Vanity of vanities; all is vanity" is rather loud. Thus what Hemingway proposed to do and what he did again seem two things, but it is doubtful that this hurts the book.

DONALD A. DAIKER ON JAKE'S ACHIEVEMENT OF SELF-MASTERY

Until a decade ago *The Sun Also Rises* had usually been interpreted as a chronicle of a lost generation, as an expression of nihilism,[1] or as a representation, in Philip Young's words, of "motion which goes no place."[2] Within the past ten years, however, some critics—though still in the minority—have discerned in Hemingway's novel a pattern of development; they have argued that at the end of the story Jake Barnes and Brett Ashley are not back where they started, that Jake has gained in self-mastery and acquired at least a measure of control in his relationship with Brett.[3] Surprisingly, even those who assert that Jake is a developing character pay scant attention to the crucial Book III.[4] Although Hemingway underscores its importance through its positioning and its brevity (it consists of but one chapter), Book III has usually been dismissed with brief mention of Jake's symbolic cleansing at San Sebastian and of his ironic statement which concludes the novel. A close reading of Book III reveals, I believe, that *The Sun Also Rises* is basically an affirmative book. Hemingway's first serious novel affirms through the characterization of Jake Barnes that man can get his money's worth in life, that he can learn how to live in the world. By the end of the story, Jake's sun has risen, and there is no suggestion that it will set.

(...)

The final and crucial test which Jake must pass before his victory is assured begins when he and Brett emerge from the coolness of the restaurant into the "hot and bright" (p. 258) streets of Madrid. Previously, Jake had always conducted himself well in the shaded and breezy settings of Bayonne, Burguete, and San Sebastian, but in the heat of Paris and Pamplona his self-control had been lost. This time, however, Jake is master of himself and the situation. In contrast to the first taxi ride in Paris,[11] Jake does not ask Brett where she would like to drive but instead chooses their destination himself, again signaling a reversal from their earlier positions but more importantly signifying that Jake knows exactly the direction in which he must proceed if he is to "finish this." As the taxi starts Jake is relaxed and confident. He sits "comfortably" (p. 258) even when Brett rests her body against his. He does not stare at Brett as he had during the first ride or as the steers had stared at the bull (p. 143). In fact, the cab ride in Madrid more closely resembles Jake's *fiacre* ride with the prostitute Georgette than the earlier drive with Brett. When Jake had gotten into the *fiacre* with Georgette he had "Settled back" until, as he relates, "She cuddled against me and I put my arm around her" (p. 15). This sequence of events is duplicated in Madrid. Having "settled back" in the taxi, Jake explains that "Brett moved close to me" and "I put my arm around her ..." (p. 258). The point is that Brett no more dominates Jake in the present that Georgette had in the past.

When the taxi turns onto the "Gran Via" (p. 258), Jake and Brett are on the "great way," the symbolic highway of life. Their responses, therefore, will reveal with high accuracy their current attitude toward each other and to life: "'Oh, Jake,' Brett said, 'we could have had such a damned good time together.'" Brett's remark is obviously inspired by self-pity. Since her affair with Romero has turned out badly—although Brett claims she made Romero leave, her crying and trembling together with her refusal to "look up" (p. 254) indicate that, as in Pamplona, she "couldn't hold him" (p. 210)—she seems to have no alternative but to go back to Mike who, she honestly admits, is her "sort of thing" (p. 255). But Brett wishes it were otherwise, and her feeling sorry for herself prompts her remark, aimed as it is both to rationalize her own failings by blaming circumstance and to evoke from Jake the sympathy and compassion she feels entitled to.

Jake, by contrast, refuses to indulge in self-pity or to share her illusions: "Ahead was a mounted policeman in khaki directing traffic. He raised his baton. The car slowed suddenly pressing Brett against me. 'Yes,' I said. 'Isn't it pretty to think so?'" (p. 259). In the closing line of the novel Jake suggests, as Mark Spilka has noted,[12] that it is foolish to believe, even had there been no war wound, that he and Brett could ever "have had such a damned good time together." But although Spilka properly recognizes the military and phallic references in the "mounted policeman in khaki" and the "raised ... baton," his conclusion that war and society have made true love impossible for those of Jake's generation oversimplifies the psychological subtleties of the situation. The reference to the khaki-clad policeman and his erect baton functions primarily to create for Jake the circumstances under which he would be most likely to revert to his old self, to lose control and to allow Brett once again to dominate him. Jake passes the ultimate and severest test of his newly-won manhood by resisting the temptation, as Brett could not, to blame the failure of their relationship upon the war or his sexual incapacity. Under maximum pressure, created physically and emotionally by Brett's "pressing ... against" him, Jake delivers in his final words the *coup de grâce* which effectively and permanently destroys all possibilities for the continuation of a romantic liaison between them.

(...)

Jake's goal of learning how to live in the world is achieved without real loss to Brett. Although she is the metaphorical bull who must receive the thrust of "Isn't it pretty to think so," Jake's final statement aims not to destroy Brett as a person but to annihilate the romantic illusion which, until recently, had made Jake an emotional cripple and which, arousing Brett's feelings of helplessness and self-pity, has permitted her psychologically to justify her promiscuity and irresponsibility. In dispelling the illusion, Jake gives Brett the opportunity for self-renewal that she herself has been unable to provide. Because her experience with Romero has "wiped out that damned Cohn" (p. 254), Brett now has the chance, thanks to Jake, of beginning afresh. The point is that even in severing the romantic ties that had united them Jake treats Brett with kindness and consideration. Remembering that Brett "can't go anywhere alone" (p. 105), Jake arranges for "berths on the Sud Express" (p. 255) so as not to leave her stranded in Madrid. Hemingway altered what had originally stood as the last line of the story—"It's nice as hell to think so"[13]—apparently because the use of profanity would indicate, as elsewhere in print, Jake's anger. Hemingway wanted to avoid any such suggestion not simply because anger would indicate Jake's lack of full self-control but also because it might imply vindictiveness, Jake's punishing Brett for having made him miserable in the past. Jake does treat Brett with irony but also with a deep sense of pity and concern.

Since manhood for Hemingway is measured not by sexual prowess but by one's ability to master his own life, Jake Barnes has demonstrated, despite his physical incompleteness, that he is fully a man in every sense that matters to Hemingway. He has mastered his life by gaining the strength and self-control to end once and for all his destructive relationship with Brett. For Jake, there will be no more nights spent in tearful longing for the might-have-been. Having known all along that "The world was a good place to buy in" (p. 153), Jake has now learned how to get his money's worth of life's pleasures and satisfactions. Most characters in *The Sun Also Rises*, of course, do not learn how to live. The bankruptcy of Mike Campbell and the foolish purchases of Bill Gorton[14] are metaphors for their inability to get their money's worth. Cohn and Brett, both of whom cry during the final scene in which they appear, obviously have not yet learned how to enjoy living. But Jake has, and it is Jake—as narrator, protagonist, and center of vision—who carries the weight of the novel and whose emotional growth and mastery of life make its conclusion quietly but deeply affirmative.

Notes

1. See, for example, James T. Farrell, *The League of Frightened Philistines* (New York: Press, 1945), pp. 20–24.

2. *Ernest Hemingway: A Reconsideration* (University Park: Pennsylvania State Univ. Press, 1966), p. 86. In *Hemingway's Craft* (Carbondale: Southern Illinois Univ. Press, 1973), Sheldon Norman Grebstein virtually repeats Young's assessment: "... the thematic movement [of *The Sun Also Rises*] is circular and at the end of the novel the protagonists are headed back to where they started" (p. 37). Numerous essays support the views of Young and Grebstein: Minda Rae Amiran, "Hemingway as Lyric Novelist," *Scripta Hieresolymitana*, 17 (1966), 292–300; William L. Vance, "Implications of Form in *The Sun Also Rises*," in *The Twenties—Poetry and Prose: 20 Critical Essays*, ed. Richard E. Langford and William E. Taylor (Deland, Florida: Everett Edwards Press, 1966), pp. 87–91; Robert W. Cochran, "Circularity in *The Sun Also Rises*," *Modern Fiction Studies*, 14 (1968), 297–305; Harold F. Mosher, Jr., "The Two Styles of Hemingway's *The Sun Also Rises*," *Fitzgerald/Hemingway Annual* (1971), pp. 262–273; and Chaman Nahal, "*The Sun Also Rises*" in *The Narrative Pattern in Ernest Hemingway's Fiction* (Rutherford, New Jersey: Fairleigh Dickinson Univ. Press, 1971), pp. 28–4.

3. The most cogent arguments are Earl Rovit, *Ernest Hemingway* (New York: Twayne, 1963), pp. 147–162, and Dewey Ganzel, "*Cabestro*

and *Vaquilla*: The Symbolic Structure of *The Sun Also Rises*," *Sewanee Review*, 76 (1968), 26–48. See also Paul B. Newman, "Hemingway's Grail Quest," *University of Kansas City Review*, 28 (1962), 295–303; Daniel J. Schneider, "The Symbolism of *The Sun Also Rises*," *Discourse*, 10 (1967), 334–342; Jackson J. Benson, *Hemingway: The Writer's Art of Self-Defense* (Minneapolis: Univ. of Minnesota Press, 1969), pp. 30–43; and Bruce L. Grenberg, "The Design of Heroism in *The Sun Also Rises*," *Fitzgerald/Hemingway Annual* (1971), pp. 274–289.

11. Although Waldhorn, p. 96, and Grebstein, p. 30, see the two taxi rides as essentially repetitive, Grenberg is clearly correct in arguing that the two rides present a "compelling contrast" (p. 285).

12. "The Death of Love in *The Sun Also Rises*," in *Twelve Original Essays on Great American Novels*, ed. Charles Shapiro (Detroit: Wayne State Univ. Press, 1958), p. 255.

13. Carlos Baker, *Ernest Hemingway: A Life Story* (New York: Scribners, 1969), p. 155.

14. In "Bill Gorton, The Preacher in *The Sun Also Rises*," *Modern Fiction Studies*, 15 (1972–73), 517–527, Morton L. Ross contends that Bill is the voice of Hemingway's code but has little to say of Bill's conduct.

MIMI REISEL GLADSTEIN ON BRETT AS HEMINGWAY'S DESTRUCTIVE INDESTRUCTIBLE WOMAN

Lady Brett Ashley is perhaps one of Hemingway's most attractive destructive women. Her androgynous appearance heightens rather than detracts from her sex appeal.[42] Though she wears her hair like a man's, her figure is described as having "curves like the hull of a racing yacht," and as Jake Barnes notes, she accentuates those curves by wearing wool jersey (SAR, 22). She does not want to adopt a traditionally feminine hairdo and remarks cryptically to Jake that one of the things wrong with her relationship with Pedro Romero was that he wanted her to grow her hair long. "He wanted me to grow my hair out. Me, with long hair. I'd look so like hell" (SAR. 242). Not only does Brett wear her hair in a boyish bob, but she also dresses in mannish clothing. She wears a "man's felt hat" and "a slipover jersey sweater and a tweed skirt" (SAR, 22). Her bisexual image is also suggested by her first appearance in the novel. She walks into the scene with a group of her homosexual friends. Jake describes them first. They too are wearing jerseys. "With them was Brett. She looked very lovely and she was very much with them" (SAR, 20). The suggestion here is that she is very much part of this group, who are men and yet, in Jake's description, mince and gesture in parodies of femininity, masculine and feminine at the same time. Another of Brett's characteristics which acts to blur sexual distinctions is her habit of calling herself "chap." She calls men chaps—"Hello, you chaps"—and then she calls herself the same in ordering a drink—"I say, give a chap a brandy and soda."

The men in her life serve her in much the same manner as religious prostitutes served Aphrodite. First they worship at her shrine; then they prostitute themselves. Jake expresses his adoration of Brett early in the story, telling her he loves her, begging her to live with him. Afterwards, he acts the pimp for her when he sets her up with Pedro Romero. Robert Cohn calls him just that. What is worse, he corrupts his *afición*; that is to say, he prostitutes his passion in order to serve hers. The price is high. At one time he had been acknowledged as one who possessed true *afición*: "When they saw that I had *afición*, and there was no password, no set questions that could bring it out, rather a sort of oral spiritual examination.... At once he [they] forgave me all my friends" (SAR, 132). Jake's clout with Montoya, the high priest of the bull cult, has been strong. When Jake prostitutes his *afición* by introducing Pedro Romero to the kind of woman who will, in the eyes of the *aficionados*, ruin him, Montoya will not even nod at Jake. When Jake leaves the hotel, Montoya does not come near him.

But Jake is not the only supplicant for the goddess's favor; more than one of her acolytes prostitutes himself for her. Robert Cohn, in the tradition of giving oneself to a stranger, offers himself to Brett, who is little more than a stranger to him. Once their weekend at San Sebastian is over, she rejects his attempts to give their relationship any special significance. His slavish devotion to her and doglike worship destroy his pride, earn him the animosity of the group, and leave him nothing. In his own words; "I've been through such hell, Jake.

Now everything's gone. Everything" (SAR, 194). The final memento he has to carry away from his encounter with Brett is a sock in the face from Pedro Romero.

Mike Campbell is another of the men who is reduced by his association with Brett while she is affected minimally. Not much can be said for Mike's character to begin with, but it is not enhanced by his association with Brett. At the end of the book he has been "cuckolded" in a sense and left alone and penniless. In fact, he is put in the position of a kept man as Brett puts up most of the money that he gives Montoya to pay their bill in Pamplona. Mike's complete degradation is shown in his final scene with Bill Gorton and Jake Barnes when he commits the unpardonable sin of gambling without money to back his bet. He has spent the last bit of money he has buying drinks and giving extravagant tips to the bartender. His complete lack of character is explored by Bill Gorton as he establishes the fact that Mike not only did not have the money to gamble with, but that he has taken all of Brett's money and still intends to sponge off yet another acquaintance when they drop him off.

Brett's role as a goddess to be worshipped is underscored in the scene with the *riau-riau* dancers. "Brett wanted to dance but they did not want her to. They wanted her as an image to dance around" (SAR, 155). Robert Cohn articulates her fatal attraction for men. "'He calls her Circe,' Mike said. 'He claims she turns men into swine.'" Figuratively she does just that. She calls Mike a swine for the way he treats Robert Cohn, responding to Jake's defense of Mike by saying, "Yes. But he didn't need to be a swine" (SAR, 181). Cohn's behavior is also swinish, as he follows Brett around, sniveling and squealing.

But Brett is not pure bitch-goddess. Certain aspects of her positive mothering qualities are also stressed. She had been a nurse during the war. She and Jake met in a hospital. She "nurses" Romero after his fistfight with Cohn. Mike Campbell comments about her mothering qualities, "She loves looking after people. That's how we came to go off together. She was looking after me" (SAR, 203). Her mothering role is underscored as she tries to maintain harmony in the group, placating the rivalrous siblings. She chides Mike when he is ugly to Cohn. Her effect on the men is analogous to the effect a strong mother has on her sons. Those who do not exert their independence and kill the domination of the Terrible Mother remain tied to her, thereby abdicating their manhood. Those who are strong, like Romero, who maintain their independence and their principles, are set free. Brett's choice to set Romero free is significant here. She chooses to leave him because she knows she is not good for him. In her depiction of her choice she stresses the difference in their ages. "I'm thirty-four, you know. I'm not going to be one of those bitches that ruins children" (SAR, 243).

But analyzing Brett in terms of bitch-goddess or Terrible Mother does not do justice to her. On one level, she does function in that capacity, but Hemingway has done much more with her character. In his original version of *The Sun Also Rises* Brett is more the heroine than she appears in the book as published.[43] She is a complex woman who has suffered much and endured. Her indestructible qualities are revealed as we become aware of her past. Jake tells Cohn that she had married Lord Ashley during the war: "Her own true love had just kicked off with the dysentery" (SAR, 39). The marriage to Ashley is disastrous. According to Mike Campbell,

Ashley, chap she got the title from, was a sailor, you know. Ninth baronet. When he came home he couldn't sleep in a bed. Always made Brett sleep on the floor. Finally, when he got really bad, he used to tell her he'd kill her. Always slept with a loaded service revolver. Brett used to take the shells out when he'd gone to sleep. She hasn't had an absolutely happy life, Brett. Damned shame, too. She enjoys things so. (SAR, 203)

Besides these two devastating personal relationships, her love affair with Jake is a source of continuing frustration because of his inability to consummate the relationship sexually.

Her personal attractiveness and desirability are not affected by her lifestyle. The men want her regardless of her behavior.

Though their self-images are dealt blows by their encounters with Brett, she remains with her illusions intact, her desirability unquestioned, and her worshippers still devoted. After he has pimped for her, corrupted his *afición*, been beat up by Cohn, disillusioned with Mike, Jake still comes the moment she beckons him. He goes to Madrid to bail her out of the hotel where she has sent Pedro Romero away though he had wanted to marry her. She claims that she would have lived with Romero if she hadn't seen that it was bad for him. Though Jake is left with next to nothing, Brett comes away from her relationship with Romero with a sense of satisfaction. Romero had loved her, wanting to marry her to prevent her from ever leaving him, but she has decided for his own good not to stay with him. "I'm not going to be that way. I feel rather good you know. I feel rather set up" (SAR, 243). Brett is able to rationalize to herself; Jake is not. He tries to escape in drink. "Don't get drunk Jake," she said. "You don't have to." Jake answers, "How do you know?" But even getting drunk does not help Jake. In the final scene Brett still retains the unshakable illusion that all of her problems would not have been if only she and Jake could have been married. Her "life lie" is safely entrenched. One has the sense that she will go forward to her next affair or marriage armed with the satisfaction of having decided not to be a bitch and the rationalization that all would have been well if only she could have married Jake. She is undaunted. Jake, however, is not so lucky. He does not even have the illusion of the lost chance with her to sustain him anymore. His final remark in the novel clearly indicates that. When Brett says to him, "Oh, Jake, we could have had such a damned good time together," his yes is qualified with "Isn't it pretty to think so?" The word "pretty" for a man like Jake says it all. Pretty is a woman's word. The notion that all would have been good, if only ..., is an attractive one, a pretty notion, but it is not sound, not substantial.

Notes

42. Hemingway's interest in sexual relativity is expressed in a novel he never published titled *Garden of Eden*. In it, the hero and heroine

experiment with sex role reversal. See Aaron Latham, "Unfinished Manuscripts Reveal a Hemingway No One Knew," *Chicago Tribune*, October 17, 1977, Sec. 3, p. 20. A number of his most appealing heroines either have mannish haircuts (Brett and Maria) or want to cut their hair to look like their lovers (Catherine). Pictures of Duff Twysdan, Hadley, and Pauline Peiffer show them all sporting mannish bobs.

43. Linda Wagner in her article about Hemingway's early heroines, "Proud and Friendly and Gently ...," reprints portions of the original first two chapters of *The Sun Also Rises*, portions deleted before publication. Wagner explains that Hemingway intended Brett to be seen as a bereaved and betrayed war victim who carries it all off with style and grace.

SCOTT DONALDSON ON BILL GORTON'S HUMOR

The most consistently funny character in *The Sun Also Rises* is Bill Gorton. Gorton is clearly modeled on the humorist Donald Ogden Stewart, who did in fact go to Pamplona in 1925 with the Hemingways, Harold Loeb, Bill Smith, Pat Guthrie, and Lady Duff Twysden. Stewart later characterized Hemingway's novel as almost reportorial in its fidelity to the events of the fiesta. He may have come to that judgment, which undervalues the book's artistry, largely as a consequence of recognizing so much of his own sometimes "crazy humor" (as he called it) in Bill Gorton's material. In fact Don Stewart, like Bill Gorton, was almost constitutionally incapable of not amusing people.[25] As Scott Fitzgerald said of him, he "could turn a Sunday school picnic into a public holiday."[26]

It was very much in character, then, for Hemingway to make Bill Gorton-Don Stewart the source of humor in the two most high-spirited chapters of the novel. These are Chapter VIII, where Bill and Jake go out to dinner in Paris, and Chapter XII, where they go fishing along the Irati. In the Paris chapter, Bill has only recently come to Europe and has just returned from a trip to Austria and Hungary. Gorton is described as "very happy." His last book had sold well. He's excited about the new crop of young light-heavyweights. He knows how to have a good time. He finds people and places wonderful. "The States were wonderful," he tells Jake. "New York was wonderful." Vienna was wonderful, he writes "Then a card from Budapest: 'Jake, Budapest is wonderful.'" Then he returns to Paris, where Jake greets him:

> "Well," [Jake] said, "I hear you had a wonderful trip."
> "Wonderful," he said. "Budapest is absolutely wonderful."
> "How about Vienna?"
> "Not so good, Jake. Not so good. It seemed better than it was." (p. 70)

A few days later, Jake and Bill meet an American family on the train to Pamplona, and the father asks if they're having a good trip. "Wonderful," Bill says (85).

This sort of highly repetitive nonsense is much funnier when spoken than on the page, as Jackson Benson has pointed out.[27] So is the famous stuffed dog discussion on the way to dinner.

(...)

Liquor obviously plays an important role in Bill's comedy. "Don [crossed out] Bill was the best of the lot," Hemingway wrote in a discarded first draft, "and he was on a hilarious drunk and thought everybody else was and became angry if they were not."[28] Alcohol not only fuels his tomfoolery, it also provides him with a potent source of the topical humor that runs through Chapter XII. "Direct action ... beats legislation," Bill remarks when Jake doctors their rum punches at the inn in Pamplona (123). Bill's voice so predominates in this Burguete section that in the first draft Hemingway tried switching to him as the first-person narrator.[29] Later he went back to Jake as narrator and straight man for Bill's repartee. Among other things, Bill makes fun of the clichés of literary criticism, Bible Belt morality, H. L. Mencken, and—especially—the Scopes trial and William Jennings Bryan's rhetoric in attacking the theory of evolution. Putting aside a hard-boiled egg and unwrapping a drumstick, Bill reverses the order "For Bryan's sake. As a tribute to the Great Commoner. First the chicken; then the egg."

"Wonder what day God created the chicken?"
"Oh," said Bill.... "how should we know? We should not question. Our stay on earth is not for long. Let us rejoice and believe and give thanks."

"Let us not doubt, brother," he adds. "Let us not pry into the holy mysteries of the hen-coop with simian fingers." Instead, "Let us utilize the fowls of the air. Let us utilize the product of the vine. Will you utilize a little, brother?" (121-2). Jake will, and so will Bill, and so will the genial Englishman named Wilson-Harris they play three-handed bridge with in the evening.

As almost every commentator on the novel has noticed, the interlude at Burguete stands in idyllic counterpoint to the sophisticated pretentiousness of Paris and the destructive passions of Pamplona. In the first draft, Hemingway let Jake and Bill confess how they felt about their lives on that fishing trip. No one can believe that he's happy, Bill remarks, but "honest to God," he is. So is Jake, he admits, "ninety percent of the time," although they're both a little embarrassed to confess it.[30] Geography has little to do with this. After their dinner at Madame Lecomte's and a long walk back to Montparnasse, Bill feels so good that he doesn't need a drink. In fact, Jake and Bill are almost always in good spirits when together, either alone or with other male companions. Don Stewart himself blamed the trouble at Pamplona in 1925 on that old "devil sex." The previous year, when he, Ernest, Hadley, John Dos Passos, Bill Bird, and Bob McAlmon had gone to Pamplona for the bullfights, the trip had been a great success.

The Sun Also Rises is the great book it is partly because of Bill Gorton's humor that directs its jibes at ideas and institutions, not human beings. In this way, Gorton provides a model of behavior that—unlike the code of the intrepid Romero—it is possible to emulate. "I did not care what it was all about," Jake reflects in one of his interior monologues. "All I wanted to know was how to live in it" (148). Gorton seems to have discovered how: without Jake's bitter sarcasm, without Mike's and Brett's disingenuous self-depreciation, without Robert's self-pity, with the best will in the world.

Not everyone, it might be objected, is temperamentally suited to enjoy life as much as Gorton, just as very few could be expected to entertain one's companions as well as he. Yet in the very subject matter of his humor, Hemingway conveys an attitude toward existence available to all. It is easiest to understand, through negation, which attitudes are invalid. The religious preach brotherhood and arrange for special privileges. The do-gooding of the Prohibitionists does no good. The know-nothingism of what are currently called "creationists" is ridiculous, and so is the catchword pedantry of the literati: "Irony and Pity." More positively, at least one basic value emerges in the subtext of such ventures into comedy as the twelve shoeshines Bill buys Mike Campbell and his persistent sales pitch for stuffed dogs.

The shoeshine scene represents Bill's humor for once gone off the rails under the tensions of Pamplona. When bootblack after bootblack polishes Mike's shoes to a higher gloss, the repetition becomes more awkward than amusing. As Mike sardonically observes, "Bill's a yell of laughter" (173). By contrast, not even a taxidermist would be likely to find the stuffed dog passage unfunny. Whether successful in inducing laughter or not, however, both scenes have a bearing on the theme of compensation in the novel.[31] Rather casually dropped into the stuffed dog dialogue is Bill's comment about "Simple exchange of values. You give them money. They give you a stuffed dog." This seemingly innocent observation underscores Hemingway's theme that the good things in life—not exclusively limited to hedonistic pleasure—have to be earned through effort and experience. It is for this reason, in part, that the shoeshine episode falls flat, since Bill's jesting contradicts that message by demeaning the low but honest trade of the bootblacks.

Notes
25. See Stewart's autobiography, *By a Stroke of Luck* (London: Paddington Press, 1975).

26. F. Scott Fitzgerald, "Reminiscences of Donald Stewart," St. Paul *Daily News*, December 11, 1921, City Life section, p. 6, in *F. Scott Fitzgerald in His Own Time: A Miscellany*, ed. Matthew J. Bruccoli and Jackson R. Bryer (Kent, Ohio: Kent State University Press, 1971), pp. 231–2.

27. Jackson J. Benson, *Hemingway: The Writer's Art of Self-Defense* (Minneapolis: University of Minnesota Press, 1969), pp. 68–9.

28. Item 202c, Hemingway Archive, Kennedy Library, Boston.

29. This experiment in shifting points of view was noted by Frederic Joseph Svoboda, *Hemingway and The Sun Also Rises: The Crafting of a Style* (Lawrence: University Press of Kansas, 1983), p. 42.

30. Item 202c, Hemingway Archive, Kennedy Library, Boston.

31. For a fuller discussion of this theme, see Scott Donaldson, "The Morality of Compensation," in *By Force of Will: The Life and Art of Ernest Hemingway* (New York: Viking, 1977), pp. 21–33.

ROBERT CASILLO ON THE OSTRACISM OF ROBERT COHN

Of all the characters of *The Sun Also Rises*, the least understood remains Robert Cohn, who becomes an object of hatred, derision, and violence at the Pamplona festival. However reprehensible Cohn may seem, any judgment of him must be made with caution. For one thing, the novel's narrator is Jake Barnes, the most influential member of the in-group from which Cohn is ostracized. Cohn is reflected through the prejudices, assumptions, and values of a character who is also his sexual rival. Even Jake admits that he had probably "not shown Robert Cohn clearly." Later, the incident at the restaurant in Pamplona defines Cohn's relation to the text in which he is represented. Jake and Bill refuse to "interpret" the Spanish menu for Cohn, who therefore must remain speechless and misunderstood. Cohn can neither represent himself nor fully speak for himself; he depends on the disclosures, distortions, and concealments of Jake Barnes.

Nonetheless, critics have no difficulty in judging Cohn. Carlos Baker and Scott Donaldson locate Cohn outside the Hemingway "code," a loose term encompassing toughness, realism, reticence, passion, honor, and *savoir-faire*. Baker's "sentimental" and romantic Cohn lacks "moral soundness" and belongs with the "neurotic" Brett Ashley and the dissipated Mike Campbell. Cohn's antitheses are Jake Barnes, tortured yet morally sound, and the bullfighter Romero, boyishly innocent but without illusions. Philip Young and Jackson J. Benson define all of the preceding characters, except Cohn, within a charmed circle more or less united in values. As for Cohn's few defenders, Robert Stevens finds some value in his Quixote-like chivalry, while Arthur Scott with some plausibility argues that Cohn is no worse than, and sometimes is superior to, his tormentors. But Scott explains neither the cultural function of the scapegoat, nor the scapegoating process, nor why this role is reserved, in *The Sun Also Rises* as elsewhere, for a Jew.

In truth, Cohn's behavior is often indistinguishable from that of Jake and the in-group. Arbitrary, hypocritical, and self-contradictory, the code affords no clear means by which to distinguish the in-group from the outsiders. Meanwhile, the in-group's solidarity is constantly threatened by jealous emulation, unacknowledged hostility, petty resentment, vain desire. Within this collapse of differences Robert Cohn plays an essential role. Far from being "other" or different, Cohn represents the code in its basest aspects of egotism, envy, and vanity; he is the projected and unacknowledged image of the confusion within the in-group. Thus the despised and supposedly parasitic Cohn is necessary to his enemies, is the novel's "pivot" and perhaps even its "center." His final ostracism permits, if only temporarily, the preservation of the in-group and its illusion of a code.

THOMAS STRYCHACZ ON JAKE AS OBSERVER

The separation of rival gesture from dramatization in "Big Two-Hearted River" resolves little for Hemingway. If Nick comports himself as a man at the sacred river, no one—scarcely even Nick himself—is there to acknowledge and validate his manhood. As another observer-figure at places of ritual, Jake Barnes shares with Nick the displacement of self into seeing. H.

R. Stoneback has argued persuasively that in *The Sun Also Rises* "Hemingway is one of the great cartographers of the *deus loci*." Yet if Jake's pilgrimage to sacred places wins spiritual peace, his psychological travail in the arenas where men demonstrate their potency is painful indeed. In particular, the key scenes where Pedro Romero performs in the bull ring before the eyes of Brett and Jake force a complete reconsideration of the usual claims about the moral, mythic, or spiritual significance of the ritual encounter, and about the psychic renewal Jake gains from it.

Watching Romero typifies Jake's role in this novel, which is firmly established as that of observer and sometime seer. "I have a rotten habit of picturing the bedroom scenes of my friends," remarks Jake in the second chapter. His impotence has transformed his friends' acts into theater and himself into director: his visionary ability appears to be at once a product of and compensation for his ability to participate in his own bedroom scenes. In another sense, Jake's "rotten habit" corresponds to that passionate witnessing which is his aficion. They "saw that I had aficion," claims Jake of Montoya's friends, as if aficion is a matter of seeing true rather than of interrogation. Several other characters comment on Jake's perceptiveness. Romero remarks: "I like it very much that you like my work.... But you haven't seen it yet. To-morrow, if I get a good bull, I will try and show it to you." And when Jake advises Montoya (to the hotel keeper's pleasure) not to give Romero the invitation from the American ambassador, Montoya asks Jake three times to "look" for him. Cast as the archetypal observer by other men who accept his evaluation of their endeavors, Jake had managed to transform observation itself into a kind of powerful witnessing. The closing scenes at Pamplona, however, will show how flimsy his authority truly is.

Approved by the adoring crowd as well as by Jake's expert appraisal, Romero's victories in the bull ring after the beating by Cohn are not only the narrative conclusion of Book II; they become the focus of Jake's own attempts to redeem his impotence. Jake perceives Romero's painful trial in the ring as a testing and affirmation of the matador's spirit— and perhaps, since Jake is another survivor of Cohn's assaults, as a vicarious affirmation of his own spirit: "The fight with Cohn had not touched his spirit but his face had been smashed and his body hurt. He was wiping all that out now. Each thing that he did with this bull wiped that out a little cleaner." Romero's process of recuperation, to Jake, depends upon a complex relationship between being watched and disavowing the watching audience (Brett in particular).

PETER GRIFFIN ON THE MODELS FOR JAKE AND BRETT

In Ernest's fictional world, there were only two "real" people: himself and the woman he loved. Everyone else was shaped, modified, distorted. Everyone else played a role, or rather had one created for them. Ernest claimed that, as an artist, he noticed—that he was objective, clinical in his observation. But everything Ernest wrote was autobiography in colossal cipher. In *The Sun Also Rises*, Ernest is most himself in Jake Barnes, the reporter with a war wound that, according to his decoration, had cost him, "more than life itself." Barnes had lost his penis in combat, but he still had his testicles. He was the quintessential twentieth-century man—alive, sensate, but without the capacity to act. Although Ernest had not been sexually mutilated in the war, he'd been rendered impotent in Pamplona. In love with Duff, passionately desirous of her, Ernest was repelled by what he saw as her vulgarities with Loeb. Yes, she was a dope addict, and needed money for her habit, money Ernest could not hope to supply. But she had acquiesced to all Loeb was, had played the romantic whore for him.

For the heroine of his novel, Ernest would use Duff. He would call her Brett Ashley, and make her a "Lady." She would have Duff's appearance and attitude, her habits and vices. There would be no mention of Duff's drug addiction—just the suggestion of a vague ennui and the mysterious need to bathe.

Ironically, Duff, in the novel, is herself an addiction—for the men she seduces. Robert Cohn calls her Circe because, he felt, she turned men into swine. Jake Barnes is "hard-boiled" with everyone, even himself, when he fights his own weakness for self-pity. But, as Robert Cohn says, Jake will play the pimp for Lady Brett. When Brett drops the bullfighter, and is alone and broke in Madrid, Jake wires he'll take the Sud Express that very night. Then he reflects: "Send a girl off with one man. Introduce her to another to go off with him. Now go and bring her back. And sign the wire with love. That was it all right. I went to lunch."

But Lady Brett Ashley is not all Duff. After reading *The Sun Also Rises*, Duff told Ernest he had "got" her pretty well, except that she hadn't "slept with the bloody bullfighter." And she hadn't. Lady Brett in *The Sun Also Rises* sleeps with the handsome young matador, Pedro Romero, because Ernest suspected Hadley wanted to make love, and perhaps had, with Cayetano Ordoñez.

JAMES NAGEL ON THE OTHER WOMEN

The scenes involving Frances Clyne are particularly resonant considering the time of Jake's narration. On one level, Robert's treatment of Frances stands in direct contrast to Jake's relationship with Brett. Jake has just suffered through the multifaceted humiliations of Pamplona, the recognition of her ignominious fling with Robert, the devastation of her seduction of Pedro Romero, and yet, when she needs him, he goes to Madrid to rescue her. Robert, in contrast, has an affair with Frances for three years, rejects her when he becomes infatuated with Brett, and sends her off to England (69). Jake is obviously the hero in this contrast of personalities, and his telling of it gives him a revenge against Robert that he never enjoys in the action of the novel.

But it is in contrast to Brett that Frances is most interesting. Whereas Brett is loving without constraints, Frances is domineering, jealous, possessive, and determined to marry Robert (5). To demonstrate these attributes, Hemingway has Jake recall a scene in 1924 in which he and Robert and Frances had dinner in Paris. When Jake mentions his plans to take Robert to Strasbourg, where a girl he knows could show them the town, Jake feels a kick under the table and switches his proposed trip to another location. Robert is unable to confront Frances directly and has to excuse himself to explain her jealousy to Jake. "I rather liked him and evidently she led him quite a life," Jake then remarks (7).

The second major scene with Frances takes place a year later, after Robert has become intrigued with Brett. In her desperation, Frances confides in Jake: "We have dreadful scenes, and he cries and begs me to be reasonable, but he says he just can't do it" (47). When the three of them meet for a drink at the Select, Frances baits Robert publicly, talking to Jake about him in the third person and openly voicing his most deplorable traits: "She turned to me with that terribly bright smile. It was very satisfactory to her to have an audience for this" (49). The cruelty of her taunts is too much for Jake, and he escapes by going into the bar: "Cohn looked up as I went in. His face was white. Why did he sit there? Why did he keep on taking it like that?" (51). Here, early in the narrative Jake is relating, Robert is discredited in romance, portrayed as insincere in his relationships and as ineffectual in dealing with women. Frances is presented in terms that contrast directly with Brett's relationship with Jake—her pained acceptance of tragedy, her independence of spirit, her pervading and undemanding love.

The prostitute Georgette Hobin functions in the novel in a similar fashion. The section that Jake narrates about her reveals his sense of irony and suggests for the first time that he is "sick" as a result of the war. Jake's encounter with Georgette allows Hemingway to introduce Jake's sexual dysfunction prior to his meeting with Brett, where the consequences are more deeply felt. It also shows Jake's need of companionship to assuage his loneliness and his ethic of fair compensation, when he leaves money for her at the dance (23). The galley proof of the novel, interestingly, contained another prostitute, a "two-hundred-pound meteoric glad girl called Flossie, who had what is known as a 'heart of gold,' lovely skin and hair and appetite, and an invulnerability to hang-overs."[22] This reference was deleted when the first two chapters were cut, leaving Georgette alone in the trade. But his evening with Georgette was not a unique experience for Jake, for he observes that he had dined with prostitutes before, although not for a long time, and had forgotten how dull it could be (16).

As a prostitute with a venereal disease, Georgette embodies the degradation of sex for money, a point underscored by her bad teeth and disastrous smile. She can be a subject of humor only as a flat character, with no real background, no explanation of how she came to Paris, no concern for what became of her. Were she presented with depth, were the situation described from her point of view, a life wasted and without promise, her characterization would be tragic, not unlike that of Jake himself. So it is important strategically that Jake not get involved with her.

(...)

The character of Georgette accomplishes several other things. For one, it demonstrates that Jake is a quick study, sensing that Georgette knows how to play her clients. When she objects to the restaurant Jake has chosen, calling it "no great thing," he responds, "Maybe you would rather go to Foyot's. Why don't you keep the cab and go on?" (16). Later, when they join the other revelers, she becomes the butt of a good deal of humor. Jake introduces her ("I wish to present my fiancée, Mademoiselle Georgette Leblanc") with great irony, not only because of the improbability of his being engaged but because the most famous chanteuse in Paris at the time was the real Georgette LeBlanc, the former mistress of Maeterlinck and also a beautiful lesbian, involved at the time with Margaret Anderson.[24] A savvy reader of the time would recognize the multiple ironies of an impotent man pretending to be engaged to a famous lesbian singer. The context emphasizes how obtuse Mrs. Braddocks is, for she not only does not get the joke but, having had it explained to her, feels it necessary to explain it to others (18). Mrs. Braddocks' lack of perception contrasts with Brett's quick assessment of the situation. One additional dimension to the Georgette scene is that the prostitute instantly objects to Frances's arch and domineering manner—a manner Robert was apparently oblivious to all along. Hence this brief scene with Georgette does a great deal for the novel, introducing the central problem with Jake, the ironic sexual humor that pervades the action, the lost-generation pathology eroding the relationships. It may well have been for this reason that when F. Scott Fitzgerald first read the manuscript, he suggested to Hemingway that it begin when Jake picks up Georgette.[25]

Another character almost totally ignored in Hemingway criticism is Edna, the extraordinarily attractive young woman Bill met at Biarritz. Mike speaks to her in terms that parallel those of the earlier scene with Brett. Mike says, "I say, she is a lovely girl. Where have I been? Where have I been looking all this while? You're a lovely thing" (180). Edna goes off with Mike and Bill, leaving Brett with Jake to confess that she is obsessed with Pedro. When Brett leaves to be with Romero, Edna functions as her surrogate in the group: Edna is there when Jake is knocked out by Robert. Later, Jake takes her to see the holding pens before the running of the bulls, as he had with Brett, and she is there in the arena when the bulls come in, screaming as the bulls enter. She wants Mike and Bill to get into the ring with them, and she enjoys the excitement of the fiesta without complications. She and Bill appear to be the only truly healthy people in the novel, although she lacks Bill's delightful humor, and she disappears into the crowd when Brett returns to the group for Pedro's final appearance. As a temporary substitute, she has no place in the group once Brett has come back. Still, Brett emerges as unique even when measured against Edna, who resembles her in many respects, for Edna has no special meaning for Jake, and he does not dwell on her personality.

Viewed in the context of the double time of the novel, and with a special concern for what would be of interest to Jake at the time of the telling, it is not surprising that his narrative should focus on Brett and the spectrum of women around her.

Jake's wound, after all, primarily transforms his relationships with women.

Notes

22. Frederic Joseph Svoboda, *Hemingway and The Sun Also Rises: The Crafting of a Style* (Lawrence: University Press of Kansas, 1983), p. 135.

24. For more background on the historic Georgette LeBlanc, see Linda Wagner-Martin, "Racial and Sexual Coding in Hemingway's *The Sun Also Rises*," *Hemingway Review* 10.20 (1991): 39–41.

25. See Svoboda 98.

DEBRA A. MODDELMOG ON SEXUAL AMBIGUITY IN THE NOVEL

With its attention to male bonding and rituals such as fishing, drinking, and bullfighting, *The Sun Also Rises* has become known as "classic Hemingway." Co-existing with these rituals is a thwarted heterosexual relationship—Jake and Brett's—a romantic situation that is also characteristic of Hemingway's fiction. The repetition of this pattern throughout Hemingway work (e.g., *A Farewell to Arms*, *For Whom the Bell Tolls*, *Across the River and Into the Trees*, *Islands in the Stream*) suggests that Hemingway felt that the intense homosociality of his fiction demanded equally intense heterosexuality to deflect suspicions that either his male characters or he had homosexual tendencies.[3] Yet a closer look at *The Sun Also Rises* reveals that Hemingway's depiction of gender and sexuality is more complex than this description allows. Ironically, in mapping out this territory of interrogation, I will draw upon the very concepts that I claim Hemingway's work problematizes (masculinity/femininity, homosexuality/heterosexuality). As Gayatri Spivak observes, "There is no way that a deconstructive philosopher can say 'something is not something' when the word is being used as a concept to enable his discourse."[4] Despite this paradox, by tracing how Hemingway's texts bring traditional significations of gender and sexuality into conflict, I hope to illustrate that Hemingway's first novel (like one of his last, *The Garden of Eden*) exposes the intellectual limitations that result when "gender" and "sexuality" are read as innocent acts of nature and as fixed binaries.

(...)

For instance, the pairing of Brett and Georgette, like the pairing of Jake and the homosexual men, is complex and multifaceted. The resemblance between the two women is underscored when Jake, half-asleep, thinks that Brett, who has come to visit him, is Georgette (32). Obviously such a correspondence reveals that both women sleep around, one because she believes it's the way she is made (55), the other because it's the way she makes a living. Yet this explanation of motives reminds us that women's outlets for their desires were closely intertwined with economic necessity in the years following World War I, even in the liberated Left Bank of Paris. As a white, heterosexually identified, upper-class woman, Brett still must depend, both financially and socially, on hooking up with one man or another. As Wendy Martin observes, "If Brett has gained a measure of freedom in leaving the traditional household, she is still very much dependent on men, who provide an arena in which she can be attractive and socially active as well as financially secure."[6]

Brett's self-destructive drinking and her attempts to distance herself from sexual role stereotyping—for example, her short hair is "brushed back like a boy's" (22) and she wears a "man's felt hat" (28)—indicate her resentment of this prescribed arrangement. Susan Gubar reminds us that many women artists of the modernist period escaped the strictures of socially defined femininity by appropriating male clothing, which they identified with freedom.[7] For such women, cross-dressing became "a way of ad-dressing and re-dressing the inequities of culturally-defined categories of masculinity and femininity" (Gubar, 479). Like Catherine Bourne of *The Garden of Eden*, Brett Ashley fits this category of women who were crossing gender lines by cross-dressing and behaving in "masculine ways." Although Brett's wool jersey sweater reveals her to be a woman, the exposure is not enough to counter the effect of her masculine apparel and appearance on the men around her. Pedro Romero's urge to both make her look more "womanly" (242) and marry her might be explained as the response of a man raised to demand clear distinctions between the gender roles of men and women. But the attempt of the more carefree Mike Campbell to convince Brett to buy a new hat (79) and to marry him suggests that Brett is dangerously close to overturning the categories upon which male and female identity, and patriarchal power, depend. The "new woman" must not venture too far outside the old boundaries.

Brett's cross-dressing conveys more than just a social statement about gender. It also evokes suggestions of the transvestism practiced by and associated with lesbians of the time (and since). As I described in Chapter 3, sexologists such as Havelock Ellis recognized the so-called mannish woman as only one kind of lesbian; nonetheless, the wearing of men's clothing by women was often viewed as sexual coding. Certainly many lesbians chose to cross-dress in order to announce their sexual preference.[8] One hint that we might read Brett's cross-dressing within this context comes in the parallel set up between her and Georgette. When Jake introduces Georgette to a group seated in the restaurant, he identifies her as his fiancée, Georgette Leblanc. As several scholars have pointed out, Georgette Leblanc was a contemporary singer and actress in Paris—and an acknowledged lesbian.[9] This association consequently deepens the symbolic relationship of Brett to Georgette, linking them in a new equation: independent/ lesbian. Brett's transvestism crosses over from gender inversion to sexual sign: not only does Brett desire the lesbian's economic and social autonomy but she also possesses same-sex desire.

In fact, Brett's alcoholism and inability to sustain a relationship might be indications not of nymphomania, with which the critics have often charged her, but of a dissatisfaction with the strictures of the male–female relationship. Brett's announcement, for example, that she can drink safely among homosexual men (22) can be taken to mean that she cannot control her own heterosexual desire, though it could also reveal underlying anxiety toward the heterosexual desire of men. Such an anxiety might be related to her abusive marriage, but that experience need not be its only source. As Brett tells Jake after the break-up with Pedro Romero, "I can't even marry Mike" (242). Of course, soon after this, she declares, "I'm going back to Mike.... He's so damned nice and he's so awful. He's my sort of thing" (243). Yet even in giving her reasons for returning to Mike, Brett reveals her inner turmoil and ambivalence. Like Mike, she is both "nice" and "awful," and the novel ends before this promised reunion occurs.

(...)

The final scene of the novel situates Jake between the raised baton of the policeman, an obvious phallic symbol and representative of the Law, and the pressure of Brett's body. Such a situation suggests that the novel does not stop trying to bridge the multiple desires of its characters. However, Brett's wishful statement—"we could have had such a damned good time together"—and Jake's ironic question—"Isn't it pretty to think so?" (247)—reveal that at least part of the failure, part of the "lostness," conveyed in the novel is that such a bridge cannot be built. The prescriptions for masculinity and femininity and for heterosexuality and homosexuality are too strong to be destroyed or evaded, even in a time and place of sexual and gender experimentation.

As my analysis suggests, to explore the fundamental equivalences implied in the dancing club scene and their reverberations throughout *The Sun Also Rises* leads to constructing a network of ambiguities and contradictions pertaining to sexuality and gender. As I admitted earlier, in creating such a construction, I have had to draw upon the very concepts that I claim Hemingway's novel calls into question (masculinity/femininity, homosexuality/heterosexuality). But by refusing to qualify or resolve the contradictions surrounding these categories and by focusing attention upon the points at which they conflict, we see that Hemingway's novel puts gender and sexuality into constant motion. Although modern society attempts to stabilize conduct and appearance as masculine or feminine, and desire as homosexual, heterosexual, or bisexual, it is still not easy to contain and categorize desire and behavior. Actions, appearance, and desire in *The Sun Also Rises* spill over the "normal" boundaries of identity and identification so that categories become destabilized and merge with one another.

Notes

3. Peter F. Cohen has recently presented an argument regarding the intense male bonds in *A Farewell to Arms* that coincides with the one I make in this chapter regarding *The Sun Also Rises*. Drawing upon Eve Sedgwick's contention that male homosocial behavior lies on the same continuum as male homosexual desire, Cohen proposes that "Rinaldi 'traffics' Catherine between himself and Frederic as a means of eroticizing his relationship with his roommate," "'I Won't Kiss You.... I'll Send Your English Girl': Homoerotic Desire in *A Farewell to Arms*," *The Hemingway Review* 15.1 (1995), 45. Although my argument posits a more comprehensive circulation of desire among the characters, Cohen has recognized that a Hemingway heroine might serve as an erotic go-between for two Hemingway heroes.

4. Gayatri Spivak, "A Response to 'The Difference Within': Feminism and Critical Theory," in *New Essays on The Sun Also Rises*, ed. Elizabeth Meese and Alice Parker (Philadelphia: John Benjamin, 1989), 213.

6. Wendy Martin, "Brett Ashley as New Woman in *The Sun Also Rises*," in *New Essays on The Sun Also Rises*, ed. Linda Wagner-Martin (Cambridge: Cambridge University Press, 1987), 71.

7. Susan Gubar, "Blessings in Disguise: Cross-Dress as Re-Dressing for Female Modernists," *Massachusetts Review* 22 (1981): 478.

8. George Chauncey observes that Havelock Ellis, like other contemporary sexologists, attempted to differentiate sexual object choice from sexual roles and gender characteristics, an attempt reflected in the distinguishing of the sexual invert from the homosexual. Chauncey also notes, however, that the sexologists were less willing to apply this distinction to women. Hence, whereas Ellis could claim that male homosexuals were not necessarily effeminate or transvestites, he was less capable of separating a woman's behavior in sexual relations from other aspects of her gender role. See Chauncey, "Sexual Inversion," 124–25. For example, although he maintained that transvestism was unrelated to homosexuality, in Ellis's own "Sexual Inversion," he still provided numerous examples of lesbian transvestites and insisted that even lesbians who dressed in "female" attire usually showed some "masculine" traits in their clothing. Ellis also believed that a keen

observer could detect "psychic abnormality" in a woman by watching her behavior. "The brusque energetic movements, the attitude of the arms, the direct speech, the inflexions of the voice, the masculine straightforwardness and sense of honor, and especially the attitude towards men, free from any suggestion either of shyness or audacity, will often suggest the underlying psychic abnormality," "Sexual Inversion in Women," *Alienist and Neurologist* 16 (1895): 153.

9. Apparently, Hemingway did not feel kindly toward Georgette Leblanc. In a letter to Ezra Pound (c. 2 May 1924), Hemingway noted that Margaret Anderson was in Paris with "Georgette Mangeuse [man-eater] le Blanc," *Ernest Hemingway: Selected Letters, 1917–1961*, ed. Carlos Baker (New York: Charles Scribner's Sons, 1981), 115. But whether he knew her personally is uncertain. According to Bertram Sarason, Margaret Anderson claimed that Leblanc had never met Hemingway and did not know her name had been mentioned in the novel. *Hemingway and The Sun Set* (Washington, D.C.: Microcard Editions, 1972), 81. Interestingly, Jake's identification of Georgette Hobin as Georgette Leblanc suggests a special kind of knowledge about prostitutes that circulated at the time. In "Sexual Inversion," Havelock Ellis remarks that the frequency of homosexuality among prostitutes is very high, especially in Paris, 210. He quotes a friend who states, "From my experience of the Parisian prostitute, I gather that Lesbianism in Paris is extremely prevalent; indeed, one might almost say normal. In particular, most of the chahut-dancers of the Moulin-Rouge, Casino de Paris, and the other public balls are notorious for going in couples, and, for the most part, they prefer not to be separated, even in their most professional moments with the other sex," 211.

LINDA WAGNER-MARTIN ON HENRY JAMES'S INFLUENCE IN THE NOVEL

At the turn of the century, one of the most popular literary forms for elite readers in both the United States and England was the expatriate novel of manners. Henry James was the author most responsible for, in effect, creating this category. One of his earliest novels, *The American*, set a successful U.S. businessman (named Christopher—with echoes of Columbus— Newman, a pointed underscoring of the promise of American democracy) adrift within a severely classed French society he had no way to understand. Similarly, in *The Portrait of a Lady*, the American woman Isabel Archer, despite her intelligence and her fortune—or, perhaps, because of them—is bested by an expatriate American man who uses European conventions to conquer her spirit. In one of James's last great novels, *The Ambassadors*, he again moved American characters into European circles where their politeness, coupled with their own sometimes foolish self-confidence, kept them from asking the right questions, from getting the information that would have, perhaps, kept them from becoming victims. Europe as predator, even when populated chiefly by other Americans, became one central trope of the expatriate novel.

Between 1907 and 1910 the New York edition of James's novels was published and many readers bought the volumes by subscription. Living in Paris, Gertrude Stein and Alice B. Toklas purchased a set of the white-covered books. James was one of the authors both Stein and her brother Leo, whom Hemingway knew separately from Gertrude through the Paris café scene, praised consistently (Jane Austen was another); and in 1917 another of Hemingway's mentors, Ezra Pound, had edited a special issue of the *Little Review* that was devoted exclusively to essays written in praise of James. There was little question about James's standing within the postwar culture of expatriates from the United States.

Having established himself as a writer of short stories, poems, and poetic vignettes, Hemingway in the mid-1920s was clearly looking for something on which to base a novel. The intertextual method shows how plausible it is that Hemingway used James's *The Ambassadors* as he shaped *The Sun Also Rises*, which Hemingway had begun as a travel diary of his and Hadley's first and second Pamplona visits. While there are a number of clear similarities, Hemingway's recalcitrance to accept James's characterizations of Americans as naive colored his approach; with the confidence of an American in his mid-twenties, able to not only belong to the elite expatriate Paris culture but to captivate it, Hemingway drew for his novel U.S. characters who were too smart to become the victims of Europeans.

No reader would ever pity Jake Barnes, even if he could not normally consummate his love. True to the narrative expectations of romance, at the end of *The Sun Also Rises* Jake almost succumbed to Brett's need; but his cryptic withdrawal, his laconic "Isn't it pretty to think so?" marked his refusal to become the romantic object. For what Hemingway most disliked about Henry James's Lambert Strether, the central "ambassador" of the impressionistic and self-conscious observation of Europe's tangled webs of friendships, adulteries, and same-sex liaisons, was his passivity. Not only was the aging and stiflingly polite Strether financially dependent on his backer/lover in the States, Mrs. Newsome, but he was emotionally enchained not so much by his love for her but by his omnipresent sense of propriety. Clouded by the admittedly provincial attitudes of Woollett, Massachusetts, Strether yet was man enough to see the values of—to admire what was "wonderful" about—Paris, the French, and Europeans in general. Caught in his obligations to Mrs. Newsome—to visit Paris and spy on her son Chad and then report back to her—Strether could still understand "freedom" (*The Ambassadors* 215).

Strether's own narrative, however, is so hedged with personal moral convictions, or what he describes as moral convictions, that he himself can never act. His conversations with Little Bilham and the perceptive and loving Maria Gostrey show that he is a man of understanding, understanding even for the most grotesque of James's American figures, Waymarsh (who, despite his own lack of sensitivity, *does* manage to act). Yet the tragedy of Strether's journey as an ambassador from Massachusetts to France is that he returns from it, marked forever by his knowledge and therefore unable to accept the role he had begun that odyssey convinced he wanted—to become Mrs. Newsome's consort, a kind of subordinate Mr. Newsome-Strether.

Determined to be seen as "modern," Hemingway stripped his Strether—Jake Barnes—of his gentility right off the bat by using the short, rough form of that character's given name, Jacob. He then stripped him of the most apparent of his sexual qualifiers, his penis, with a kind of ironic commentary on the use normally-equipped male characters might not have made of their God-given rights as men. (The fact that *The*

Sun Also Rises contains a dialogue devoted to Jake's impotence juxtaposed with comments about what a good writer Henry James is, despite his apparent emasculation, lends a writerly subtext to this discussion; perhaps more important is that the dialogue occurs between Jake and Bill Gorton, the two closest male friends in Hemingway's work.) Hemingway then wrote an entire novel around what might be seen as a deftly embroidered casting and recasting of Lambert Strether's admonition to Little Bilham:

> ... don't forget that you're young—blessedly young; be glad of it on the contrary and live up to it. Live all you can; it's a mistake not to. It doesn't so much matter what you do in particular, so long as you have had your life. If you haven't had that what *have* you had? (*The Ambassadors* 215)

Taking his cue from one of James's best-known passages, then, in *The Sun Also Rises*, Hemingway attempts to force a festival of experience—bullfighting, traveling, fishing, bicycle racing, eating, drinking, church going, dancing, loving, fighting, drinking, eating, and, that most American of themes, searching for (and perhaps finding) the self—into one short novel. And rather than create a mellowed-by-experience observer like James's Lambert Strether, Hemingway gives us the brash (but still writerly, still sensitive) journalist, Jake Barnes. Impatient with Robert Cohn's literary romanticism—that he find a better country, find a better woman, write a better book, Jake demands that people find their pleasures where they are, realize what is "wonderful" about their current lives, and stop the endless café talk about what might be possible. As Jake answers Cohn, even to the point of having to fight with him, so *The Sun Also Rises* answers *The Ambassadors*.

The most important difference, of course, is that Jake has not been *sent* to Europe by anyone. Even though Hemingway was at that time living off his first wife Hadley's inheritance, he could believe that he was independent because he was convinced that he would eventually earn his way by writing. *The Sun Also*

Rises makes clear that there are no puppet strings attached to Jake Barnes, just as Hemingway's first novel attempts to cut whatever strings of influence the young writer might have felt were being attached to him. It is no accident that his parodic novel *The Torrents of Spring* appeared just before this one, for in his ill-conceived take-off on both Sherwood Anderson and Gertrude Stein, Hemingway reminded the literary world that he was an original, that he did not like his work being coupled with that of either Stein or Anderson. *The Sun Also Rises* was his gesture of farewell to both of those writers, as well as to the meditative American novel, the interminable dialogic text that pondered, pondered, pondered. Anderson's *Poor White* as well as Stein's *The Making of Americans*, which Hemingway had typed some parts of in order to publish it in *transatlantic review*, were both in the Jamesian mode.

But even as he tried to leave the stylistic and narrative model of the long novel of manners, Hemingway found much about the form useful. He too, like James, wanted to vaunt his intimate knowledge of France (and Spain), knowledge philosophical and religious as well as anthropologic and geographic. He also wanted to champion the innocence of Americans who were less cynical and jaded than their European counterparts. And he especially wanted to impress his readers with the assurance of his own, Jake Barnes's own, sophistication. While the avuncular James radiated his cosmopolitanism, the handsome, intentionally rugged, young American writer searched for ways to exude that same quality.

More directly, from James's *The Ambassadors* Hemingway took the sexuality and centrality of Madame de Vionnet; at thirty-eight, she is the seductively beautiful prototype of the *femme du monde*, the civilizing woman. Unfortunately, in James's novel, she is a woman who loved unwisely. While Brett Ashley transmuted the gentility of de Vionnet into a sexual energy that James left to the reader's imagination, a more recognizable Hemingway *femme du monde* character appeared later as Catherine Barkley in his *A Farewell to Arms*. But there were uses to be made of de Vionnet in Brett as well, and what moved James's figure into the "modern" in Hemingway's first novel was Brett's utter lack of hypocrisy. Although she slept with many men, she did not care who knew it. She thought sexual experience with her might be "good" for them, and until she fell in love with the very young Pedro Romero (which makes her a closer parallel with Madame de Vionnet), she was usually unharmed by her liaisons.

What was perhaps most "modern" about Brett Ashley was her androgynous character. Like Jake, she ate well, drank a lot, enjoyed the bullfights, wanted to be at the center of the vigor of life. In contrast to the veiled and mysterious sexuality of Madame de Vionnet, Brett's female being came closer to the male in its aggression, its lack of subtlety, and its visible appetites (see Barlowe, Elkins [both in this volume]). Or perhaps, if the reader follows the lead of Mark Spilka in his important book, the issues of femaleness and maleness were also blurred enough for Hemingway that he was borrowing more from the character of Strether—especially Strether in his relation to Little Bilham—than *The Sun Also Rises* made clear. The mirror scene, in which Jake acknowledges and mourns his neutering, becomes central in the reader's determining what role Jake is really to la in Hemingway's tapestry.

In point of structure, *The Sun Also Rises* is *The Ambassadors* writ modern. A group of men come together in Europe, their lives defined to a great extent by their friendships. Their action consists largely of determining what their role is in relation to the female energy of the culture—whether that energy be provided by Madame de Vionnet or Brett Ashley or Paris itself. And there are complicating negative sources of female energy—Frances, Mrs. Newsome, Sarah Pocock (to some extent), Woollett; the presence of these entities makes the positive sources stand out brilliantly. In *The Sun Also Rises*, typical of the commonness of the male center, Jake, male friendships sort themselves out through battle, in a bloodshed that would be unseemly in James's text (especially in Gloriani's garden). In *The Ambassadors*, the violence remains hidden under the facade of socially acceptable behavior, but its damage is done nonetheless. That the old sculptor, Gloriani, shares his wisdom and his own sexual energy during his "queer old" garden party, his welcoming face offering the bemused Strether an "open letter in a foreign tongue" (197, 99), gives depth to Hemingway's characterization of the Spanish mentor, Montoya, whose knowledge of the mysterious Spanish culture with its rites and rituals similarly attracts Jake. By the 1940s Hemingway would return to the idea of glorious gardens and same-sex friendships and pursue issues of sexuality and moral loyalties more fully.

It might also be said, coming to the end of both *The Sun Also Rises* and *The Ambassadors*, that Lambert Strether was not the only male protagonist who relinquished what he could have loved so that he could return, in a sense, to his natively moral beginnings.

Works by Ernest Hemingway

Three Stories and Ten Poems, 1923.

In Our Time, 1924.

In Our Time: Stories, 1925.

The Torrents of Spring, 1926.

Today Is Friday, (pamphlet), 1926.

The Sun Also Rises, 1926.

Men Without Women, 1927.

A Farewell to Arms, 1929.

Death in the Afternoon, 1932.

God Rest You Merry Gentlemen, (pamphlet), 1933.

Winner Take Nothing, 1933.

Green Hills of Africa, 1935.

To Have and Have Not, 1937.

The Spanish Earth, (film transcript) 1938.

The Fifth Column and the First Forty-nine Stories, 1938.

For Whom the Bell Tolls, 1940.

Men at War: The Best War Stories of All Time (editor), 1942.

Voyage to Victory: An Eye-witness Report of the Battle for a Normandy Beachhead, 1944.

The Portable Hemingway, Ed, Malcolm Cowley, 1944

Selected Short Stories, c, 1945.

The Essential Hemingway, 1947.

Across the River and into the Trees, 1950.

The Old Man and the Sea, 1952.

The Hemingway Reader, Ed, Charles Poore, 1953.

Two Christmas Tales, 1959.

Collected Poems, 1960.

The Snows of Kilimanjaro and Other Stories, 1961.

The Wild Years, Ed, Gene Z, Hanrahan, 1962.

A Moveable Feast, 1964.

By-Line: Ernest Hemingway: Selected Articles and Dispatches of Four Decades, Ed, William White, 1967.

The Fifth Column and Four Stories of the Spanish Civil War, 1969.

Ernest Hemingway, Cub Reporter, Ed, Matthew J, Bruccoli, 1970.

Islands in the Stream, 1970.

Ernest Hemingway's Apprenticeship: Oak Park 1916-1917, Ed, Matthew J, Bruccoli, 1971.

The Nick Adams Stories, 1972.

88 Poems, Ed, Nicholas Gerogiannis, 1979, 1992 (as *Complete Poems*).

Selected Letters 1917-1961, Ed, Carlos Baker, 1981.

The Dangerous Summer, 1985.

Dateline, Toronto: Hemingway's Complete Toronto Star Dispatches, 1920–1924, Ed, William White, 1985.

The Garden of Eden, 1986.

Complete Short Stories, 1987.

Remembering Spain: Hemingway's Civil War Eulogy and the Veterans of the Abraham Lincoln Brigade, Ed, Cary Nelson, 1994.

True at First Light, 1999.

Annotated Bibliography

Baker, Carlos. *Hemingway: the Writer as Artist*. Princeton: Princeton University Press, Fourth Edition, 1973.

Carlos Baker is prominent among Hemingway scholars and biographers. The eighth printing of this volume appeared in 1990. Each edition drew on newly published work in Hemingway's lifetime, posthumously published titles, and newly discovered biographical information. Hemingway famously disdained and discredited attempts at his biography and explication of his work, but Baker's work is widely believed to be among the most authentic. The focus here is not on biographical details for their own sake but as indicators of what influenced Hemingway's development as a prominent writer in American society.

Bakker, Jan. *Ernest Hemingway in Holland, 1925–1981: A Comparative Analysis of the Contemporary Dutch and American Critical Reception to his Work*. Amsterdam: Editions Rodopi B. V., 1986.

The lengthy title is explicit about the book's focus. Hemingway was, and remains, a popular writer in The Netherlands. Bakker moves chronologically through all the reviews of the major works in both countries and analyzes the cultural differences they reflect. About *The Sun Also Rises*, Bakker notes the Dutch reviewers tended not to value seriously the dilemmas faced by the expatriates. He speculates that Dutch neutrality in World War I may be one explanation.

Donaldson, Scott, ed. *The Cambridge Companion to Ernest Hemingway*. Cambridge: Cambridge University Press, 1996.

Each edition in the *Cambridge Companion* series offers an excellent range of commentary on major writers. This study begins with the editor's look at the consequence for Hemingway readers of the writer's pursuit of public fame at the same time he was working for literary achievement. Since Hemingway committed suicide, it is especially important to establish a reliable version of his life to juxtapose against the myths that he deliberately cultivated. The edition includes commentary on Hemingway's most important fiction.

Gladstein, Mimi Reisel. *The Indestructible Women in Faulkner, Hemingway, and Steinbeck*. Ann Arbor, Michigan: UMI Research Press, 1986.

The author attempts here a thoughtful appraisal of three major American writers, all male, who created strong females in their cast of memorable characters. This updated 1986 version incorporates into the 1974 edition information and insight about these writers that has been produced in the intervening years. The author's motive appears less strident than that found in some other feminist writing about male authors. In her Preface, Gladstein states explicitly that although she does not write to absolve her writers of sexist stereotyping, she recognizes that they wrote without benefit of consciousness-raising efforts devoted to these issues and that they did in fact create women with admirable and enduring qualities. In her section on Hemingway, Gladstein reviews some of the prevailing attitudes about Hemingway on women, including the extremes of woman as "bitch goddess" and woman as "corn goddess"—images both destructive and nurturing. There is also speculation about the influence of Grace Hall Hemingway on her son. About Brett Ashley, Gladstein is sympathetic, seeing her as uncontainable by either category.

Kert, Bernice. *The Hemingway Women*. New York: W. W. Norton & Company, 1983.

Hemingway had four wives and one high-minded and talented mother. Although he is widely believed to have had antagonistic or inadequate views about women, he spent much time in the company of many. The wives came and left with varying levels of resentment. Kert undertakes this study to focus exclusively on the women in Hemingway's life, including those he attracted and did not marry. An account of the response Hemingway's mother had to her son's first novel is especially interesting.

Killinger, John. *Hemingway and the Dead Gods: A Study in Existentialism*. Lexington: University of Kentucky Press, 1960.

This interesting study establishes an intellectual connection between the major Existentialist writers and Hemingway's novels. The concepts of *nada*—nothingness and meaninglessness—and courage in the face of death put forward by German theologian Paul Tillich and French writer Jean-Paul Sartre are particularly illuminating for any understanding of what animates and motivates the characters in *The Sun Also Rises*.

Lewis, Robert W. Jr. *Hemingway on Love*. Austin: University of Texas Press, 1965.

Lewis places less emphasis on the Hemingway-as-his-own-hero theory and looks instead at the overlapping but distinct ideas of Eros and Agape as they influence the development of Hemingway's characters.

Moddelmog, Debra A. *Reading Desire: In Pursuit of Ernest Hemingway*. Ithaca and London: Cornell University Press, 1999.

This complex approach to Hemingway the man and his work draws from poststructuralist perspectives, feminist theory, and recent revelations about Hemingway's personal life. Much attention is given to the issues of androgyny and sexuality. Moddelmog is well-versed in the main readings of Hemingway that precede her and she challenges many of the older perspectives. She offers a lengthy reading of Hemingway's posthumously published and relatively less well-known novel, *The Garden of Eden* (1986).

Nagel, James, ed. *Collected Essays on Ernest Hemingway's "The Sun Also Rises."* New York: G. K. Hall & Co., 1995.

Editor and Hemingway scholar James Nagel's Introduction is a succinct gathering of early reviews for historical perspective and a brief discussion of several critical studies on the novel put forth over the years including some that Nagel finds inadequate.

The bulk of the essays are reprints from earlier studies. Nagel notes that the founding of the Hemingway Collection at the JFK Library in Boston in 1980 made possible new scholarship and theory which this editor draws on, as do some of the contributors.

Reynolds, Michael S. The Sun Also Rises: *a Novel of the Twenties*. Boston: Twayne Publishers, 1988.

The book begins with a chronology of Hemingway's life and work. Reynolds's study of *The Sun Also Rises* is more than a literary analysis. He provides historical information about World War I and its aftermath, Prohibition, the rise of the KKK and fundamentalism in religion, and the Scopes Monkey Trial—all of which are mentioned, directly or indirectly, in the novel. Reynolds begins his discussion of Jake Barnes with a reference to a film version of *Hamlet* which began, "This is the story of a man who could not make up his mind," and suggests the same could be observed about Hemingway's narrator. An unusual and welcome feature is the brief commentary Reynolds offers at the end of his study about why we like and feel connected to the sad and often wayward characters Hemingway has given us.

Rovit, Earl. *Ernest Hemingway*. New York: Twayne Publisher, Inc., 1963.

Rovit is one of many scholars attempting to establish Hemingway the man from his public personas. In the Preface he confesses to failing in this effort and goes on to treat the life and the work as an entity with many overlapping lines. Chapter Six takes up the issue of time, which for Hemingway consisted of two categories: the long expanses of geological time and the immediate moments of consciousness his characters move through. After establishing his methods for approaching Hemingway, Rovit applies these to a detailed study of *The Sun Also Rises* in Chapter Seven. Readers interested in the Hemingway code of the hero will find much of interest here. A brief chronology is included.

Svoboda, Henric Joseph. *Hemingway's "The Sun Also Rises": The Crafting of a Style*. Lawrence: University Press of Kansas, 1983.

This study provides a comprehensive look at the multiple drafts and revisions Hemingway made to *The Sun Also Rises*. Background information about the first two titles, *Fiesta* and *Lost Generation*, is included. Svoboda discusses Hemingway's often acute sensitivity to the commentary his work attracted from critics in part because it expands our knowledge of the writer's personality and character.

Wagner-Martin, Linda, ed. *A Historical Guide to Ernest Hemingway*. Oxford and New York: Oxford University Press, 2000.

This relatively recent study takes on Hemingway as an American icon with appeal for both scholars and less-educated Americans. She laments that the early study of Hemingway in high schools was limited to the short stories which perpetuated a sense of his being a writer of simple adventures. She selects the contributions for the book with an interest in making Hemingway's complexity and achievement more available to the general public. Of special interest is an essay by Susan Beegel, "Hemingway as a Naturalist," that links the writer's early experiences in nature with his lifelong reverence for the land in all parts of the world. Beegel suggests Hemingway be seen as an early ecologist. The volume offers a detailed chronology with accompanying photographs.

Wagner-Martin, Linda, ed. *New Essays on "The Sun Also Rises."* Cambridge: Cambridge University Press, 1987.

New Essays, published 60 years after *The Sun Also Rises* appeared, was organized around the belief that the standard ways of reading the novel were substantial and insightful but inadequate to the richness of the text which has persisted in a fresh way for each new generation of readers. Some of the contributors have written on Hemingway before but offer for this volume readings based on new developments in literary theory. Other contributors are writing on Hemingway for the first time benefiting from recent discoveries about Hemingway's life and the establishment of the feminist literary perspective.

White, William, ed., *The Merrill Studies in "The Sun Also Rises."* Columbus, Ohio: The Charles E. Merrill Publishing Company, 1969.

This older study has two sections. The first gathers some of the earliest reviews of SAR from major newspapers and literary magazines. The second includes some of the early commentary on the novel by critics like Carlos Baker and Philip Young who went on to make major contributions to the large and well-established collection of Hemingway criticism.

Wylder, Delbert F. *Hemingway's Heroes.* Albuquerque: University of New Mexico Press, 1969.

In this study, Wylder diverges from the majority of Hemingway critics who have emphasized the common features of a Hemingway "hero code" to focus on the distinctive features in each novel that instead reflect Hemingway's evolving and maturing perspective.

Young, Philip. *Ernest Hemingway: A Reconsideration.* University Park and London: Pennsylvania State University Press, 1966.

Philip Young distinguished himself as a Hemingway critic with his theory that the experience of being wounded in World War I had a lasting effect on Hemingway and profoundly influenced his writing. Young's study reviews the development of two Hemingway heroes: one who has sustained some kind of traumatic wound—not always physical—that informs the rest of his life, and another who has developed and passes on to others a code of right living. This code is akin to an existential posture that enables living in adverse conditions with honor and meaning. Hemingway resisted this interpretation of his work and opposed the book's publication.

Contributors

Harold Bloom is Sterling Professor of the Humanities at Yale University. He is the author of 30 books, including *Shelley's Mythmaking, The Visionary Company, Blake's Apocalypse, Yeats, A Map of Misreading, Kabbalah and Criticism, Agon: Toward a Theory of Revisionism, The American Religion, The Western Canon,* and *Omens of Millennium: The Gnosis of Angels, Dreams, and Resurrection. The Anxiety of Influence* sets forth Professor Bloom's provocative theory of the literary relationships between the great writers and their predecessors. His most recent books include *Shakespeare: The Invention of the Human,* a 1998 National Book Award finalist, *How to Read and Why, Genius: A Mosaic of One Hundred Exemplary Creative Minds, Hamlet: Poem Unlimited, Where Shall Wisdom Be Found?,* and *Jesus and Yahweh: The Names Divine.* In 1999, Professor Bloom received the prestigious American Academy of Arts and Letters Gold Medal for Criticism. He has also received the International Prize of Catalonia, the Alfonso Reyes Prize of Mexico, and the Hans Christian Andersen Bicentennial Prize of Denmark.

Portia Williams Weiskel has taught English and journalism in both high school and adult education atmospheres, and has done freelance copyediting for numerous colleges. Her publications include writings on Joyce, Tolstoy, and Wilder.

Carlos Baker was Woodrow Wilson Professor of English at Princeton University. He wrote about Shelley, Faulkner, and Emerson, but was most closely associated with Hemingway. His *Hemingway: The Writer as Artist* concentrated on the fiction; he waited until Hemingway died to write his famous biography in which he relied on material authorized for his use by Hemingway's widow, Mary Hemingway. Hemingway actively disliked any attempts at writing his biography, but Baker was able to correspond with him from the early 1950s until the writer's death in 1961.

Mark Spilka was professor of English at Brown University. He has received high praise for his work on the novel in general and specifically for work on D. H. Lawrence, Kafka, Dickens, Virginia Woolf, and Hemingway. He published *Hemingway's Quarrel with Androgyny* in 1990. In 1997 he published *Eight Lessons in Love: A Domestic Violence Reader*, a critical study of the fictional treatment of domestic violence.

Earl Rovit teaches English at the City University of New York. In addition to his work on Hemingway he has written novels that have been compared to those of Joyce, Malamud, and Pirandello.

Philip Young lectured on American literature in India through the State Department in 1957. His teaching career took place mainly at Pennsylvania State University. His last appointment was as a fellow in the Institute for Arts and Humanistic Studies. Besides his work on Hemingway, Young also wrote about Melville and Hawthorne.

Donald A. Daiker is an English educator whose most recent position was at Miami University in Oxford, Ohio. He is a member of The Hemingway Society and The Melville Society and has worked for the Educational Testing Services at Princeton.

Mimi Reisel Gladstein is associate dean of liberal arts and professor of English at the University of Texas in El Paso. Besides her work on Hemingway, Faulkner, and Steinbeck, she has written on Ayn Rand and is editor of *Feminist Interpretations of Ayn Rand*.

Scott Donaldson is the Louise G. T. Cooley Professor of English, Emeritus. In addition to his work on Hemingway, *By Force of Will: The Life and Art of Ernest Hemingway*, Donaldson has written biographies of Fitzgerald, John Cheever, and Archibald MacLeish.

Michael S. Reynolds taught English at North Carolina State University in Raleigh. He is especially known for being a literary sleuth in pursuit of Ernest Hemingway. He concentrated on finding the truth about the myths circulating around the writer, often ones generated deliberately by the author himself. Reynolds discovered, for example, that at least for some of his stories, Hemingway did research for his characters' lives. Hemingway claimed that he wrote only about what he personally knew. Reynolds is also identified with the anti-psychoanalytic trend in Hemingway studies. To gather research about Hemingway's life in Havana he applied for a visa but was blocked from entering the country. He wrote several studies of different phases of Hemingway's life and the Twayne series, *The Sun Also Rises: A Novel of the Twenties*.

Linda Patterson Miller teaches English at Pennsylvania State University in Abington. She has also served as a consultant for PBS.

James Nagel is J. O. Eidson Distinguished Professor of American Literature at the University of Georgia. In addition to his work on Hemingway, Nagel has written on Sarah Orne Jewett, Steinbeck, Stephen Crane, and Joseph Heller. In 1989 he edited with Henry Serrano Villard *Hemingway in Love and War: The Lost Diaries of Agnes Von Kurowsky*, material from which served as a source for the 1996 film about Hemingway, *In Love and War*.

Debra A. Moddelmog is a professor of English at Ohio State University in Columbus.

Linda Wagner-Martin is well known for her work on Sylvia Plath. In addition to her work on Hemingway, she has written about several female American writers including Joyce Carol Oates, Denise Levertov, and Barbara Kingsolver.

Acknowledgments

"Marital Tragedy," *The New York Times Book Review*, October 31, 1926. © 1926, *The New York Times*. Reprinted by permission.

Carlos Baker. From *Hemingway* © 1952 Princeton University Press, 1956 2nd Edition, 1980 renewed in author's name. Reprinted by permission of Princeton University Press.

Donald A. Daiker, "The Affirmative Conclusion of The Sun Also Rises," McNeese Review, 21, 1974-75. Used by permission of Donald A. Daiker.

Mimi Reisel Gladstein, from *The Indestructible Woman in Faulkner, Hemingway, and Steinbeck*, UMI Research Press, 1986. Used by permission of Mimi Reisel Gladstein.

Scott Donaldson, "Humor in The Sun Also Rises," *New Essays on* The Sun Also Rises, Cambridge University Press, 1987. Reprinted with the permission of Cambridge University Press.

Linda Patterson Miller, "Brett Ashley: The Beauty of It All", *Critical Essays on Ernest Hemingway's The Sun Also Rises*, Simon & Schuster, 1995. Used by permission of Linda Patterson Miller.

Philip Young, from *Ernest Hemingway: A Reconsideration*, pp. 86-88. Copyright © 1966 by Philip Young. Published by The Pennsylvania State University Press. Reproduced by permission of the publishers.

James Nagel, "Brett and the Other Women in The Sun Also Rises," *The Cambridge Companion to Hemingway*, ed. By Scott Donaldson, Cambridge University Press, 1996. Reprinted with the permission of Cambridge University Press.

Index

A

Aficionados, 34–35, 55
Agassiz, Louis, 10
Aimlessness, loss and, 20
Alcohol
    Bill Gorton and, 70
    Brett and, 84–85
    as defense, 20
The Ambassadors (James),
    comparison with, 86–92
Ambiguity, sexuality and, 81–85
The American (James), 86
American Red Cross, 10–11
Amorality, 27–28. *See also* Morality
Anderson, Margaret, 79
Anderson, Sherwood, 11, 90
Anti-Semitism
    Bill Gorton and, 17, 29
    Robert Cohn and, 22
Aphrodite, prostitutes and, 65
Archer, Isabel (*Portrait of a Lady*),
    86
Asceticism, 58
Ashley, Brett
    Bloom on, 7, 8
    character overview, 16–17
    Count Mippipopolous and, 27
    destructiveness of, 44–46, 64–68
    Duff Twysden as, 76–77
    model for, 76–77
    as "new woman", 23–24
    Pedro Romero and, 43–45
    self-renewal and, 62–63
    sexuality and, 28, 83–84, 90–91

B

Barnes, Jake
    Bloom on, 8
    bullfighting and, 35–36, 50, 55
    character overview, 16
    dignity and, 13

loss and, 43–44, 46, 47–48
    model for, 76–77
    as observer, 74–76
    ostracism of Robert Cohn and,
        73–74
    perspective of, 21–22
    self-mastery of, 59–63
    sexuality and, 16, 22, 24–25,
        46–47, 88–89
    strength of, 25–26, 36, 46,
        62–63
Betrayal, 38
Bigotry, Bill Gorton and, 17
"Big Two-Hearted River", 74
Bill
    anti-Semitism of, 17, 29
    character overview, 17
    humor of, 48, 69–72
Boredom
    Hemingway and, 11
    marriage and, 26
    Waste Land (Eliot) and, 20
Brett
    Bloom on, 7, 8
    character overview, 16–17
    Count Mippipopolous and,
        27
    destructiveness of, 44–46
    Duff Twysden as, 76–77
    as indestructible woman, 64–68
    model for, 76–77
    as "new woman", 23–24
    Pedro Romero and, 43–45
    self-renewal and, 62–63
    sexuality and, 28, 83–84, 90–91
Bryan, William Jennings, 70
Bullfighting
    Hemingway and, 35–36
    honor and, 17, 18
    Jake and, 50
    life and, 57

Pedro Romero and, 37–38, 41
values and, 55

C

Campbell, Mike
  Brett and, 16, 18, 29
  character overview, 18
  degradation of, 66
  lack of decency of, 35–36, 38–39
Catholicism. *See also* Religion
  pilgrimages and, 29–30
  values and, 32
Circe, 35, 44, 66
Clyne, Frances
  character overview, 18, 21
  possessiveness of, 19, 26, 77–78
Cohn, Robert
  Brett and, 16, 24, 32–33, 35–36
  as broken man, 40
  character overview, 17
  Jake's view of, 21
  ostracism of, 73–74
  prostitution of, 65–66
Collier's, 12
Creationism
  humor and, 70, 72
  influence of, 14
Cynicism as defense, 20

D

Death
  certainty of, 15
  of love, 22, 56, 61–62, 78–79
  love and, 30
Decency, lack of, 36
Degradation
  Mike and, 66
  violence and, 54–57
Depression, Hemingway and, 12
Despair, Bloom on, 8–9
Destructiveness, Brett Ashley and, 44–46, 64–68
Detachment, Jake and, 29
Development, self-mastery and, 59–63

De Vionnet, Madame (*The Ambassadors*), 90–91
Dialogue, Hemingway and, 30–31
Discomfort, readers and, 36
Duff. See Twysden, Duff

E

Ecclesiastes, 8, 14
Edna, 80
Elegy, Bloom on, 8
Epigraphs, 14, 56
Escape, social distractions as, 22
Evolution, 14
Expatriates, cultural mood of, 20–21

F

Facts, Hemingway and, 52–53
A Farewell to Arms, 11
Feminism, Brett and, 16–17
Fisher King (*Waste Land*), 7, 58
Frances
  character overview, 18, 21
  possessiveness of, 19, 26, 77–78

G

Georgette
  Brett and, 83–84
  character of, 18–19, 78–80
  Jake and, 22–23
Goddess, Brett as, 64–68
Gorton, Bill
  anti-Semitism of, 17, 29
  character overview, 17
  humor of, 48, 69–72
Gratitude, religion and, 33–34
The Great Gatsby (Fitzgerald), 7–8, 24

H

Hair, Brett and, 64
Heart of Darkness (Conrad), 7
Hedonism, as defense, 20
Hemingway, Ernest
  Bloom on, 8

Jake as, 76–77
life of, 10–12
reality in writings of, 50–53
Hemingway Review, 12
Heroism
   denigration of, 35–36
   Hemingway and, 10–11
   Jake and, 16, 77
   Pedro Romero and, 37–38, 57
   Robert Cohn and, 17
Homosexuality
   ambiguity and, 81–85
   Brett and, 28, 64–65
   disdain of, 23–24
Honor, Pedro Romero and, 17
Humming, 37
Humor
   Bill Gorton and, 48, 69–72
   Georgette and, 79
   use of, 34

I

Idealism, humor and, 71
Impotence. See Sexuality
Institutions, humor and, 71
Intimacy, taxis and, 46–47

J

Jake
   Bloom on, 8
   bullfighting and, 35–36, 50, 55
   character overview, 16
   dignity and, 13
   loss and, 43–44, 46, 47–48
   model for, 76–77
   as observer, 74–76
   ostracism of Robert Cohn and,
      73–74
   perspective of, 21–22
   self-mastery of, 59–63
   sexuality and, 16, 22, 24–25,
      46–47, 88–89
   strength of, 25–26, 36, 46,
      62–63
James, Henry, influence of, 86–92

K

Kansas City Star, 10
Key West, Hemingway and, 12

L

Lausanne Peace Conference, 11
LeBlanc, Georgette, 79, 84
Life
   enjoyment of, 63
   self-pity and, 60–61
Lincoln, Abraham, 7–8
Literary criticism, humor and, 70
Loss
   Jake and, 46, 47–48
   of morality, 58
   war and, 20, 27–28, 49–50
Love
   death of, 22, 56, 61–62, 78–79
   impermanence of, 15, 30
In Love and War (Attenborough),
   11

M

The Making of Americans (Stein), 90
Marriage, tedium and, 26
Mike
   Brett and, 16, 18, 29
   character overview, 18
   degradation of, 66
   lack of decency of, 35–36, 38–39
Military experience of Hemingway,
   10–11
Mippipopolous (Count)
   amorality of, 27–28
   character overview, 18
Money, Mike Campbell and, 18
"Monkey Trial", influence of, 14.
   See also Scopes trial
Montoya, 18, 65
Morality
   The Ambassadors (James) and, 88
   Count Mippipopolous and,
      27–28
   humor and, 70

loss of, 58
Montoya and, 18
Mortality, Bloom on, 8

N
Narration
  Bloom on, 7
  Hemingway and, 50–53
  Jake and, 16, 23, 43
Nature
  enjoyment of, 31–32, 34
  Hemingway and, 10
  religion and, 14
"New woman", Brett as, 23–24
New York Times Book Review,
  49–50
Nihilism, 13, 59
Nineteenth Amendment, influence
  of, 14
Nostalgia, Bloom on, 8

O
Objectivity, possibility of, 21–22
Observation, Jake and, 74–76
Old Man and the Sea, 12
Ostracism of Robert Cohn, 73–74

P
Paranoia, Hemingway and, 12
Pedro
  Brett and, 17, 43–45, 67–68
  bullfighting and, 41
  character overview, 17
  as hero, 37–38, 57
  observation of, 75–76
Pilgrimages, 29–30, 74
Place, sense of, 51–52
Polo shirts, 40
Poor White (Anderson), 90
The Portrait of a Lady (James),
  86
Possessiveness, Frances and, 19,
  26, 77–78
Pound, Ezra, 11, 86
Prejudice

Bill Gorton and, 17, 29
Robert Cohn and, 22
Prohibition, 20
Prostitutes
  death of love and, 22, 78–79
  Georgette as, 18–19
  men and, 65
Purple Land, 21

R
Red Cross, 10–11
Religion
  failure of, 58
  gratitude and, 33–34
  Hemingway and, 29–30
  humor and, 72
  men and, 65
  nature and, 14
  pilgrimages and, 29–30
  values and, 32
Richardson, Hadley, 11
Robert
  Brett and, 16, 24, 32–33, 35–36
  as broken man, 40
  character overview, 17
  Jake's view of, 21
  ostracism of, 73–74
  prostitution of, 65–66
Romanticism
  Jake and, 56, 62
  Robert Cohn and, 21, 26
Romero, Pedro
  Brett and, 17, 43–45, 67–68
  bullfighting and, 41
  character overview, 17
  as hero, 37–38, 57
  observation of, 75–76
Roosevelt, Theodore, 11

S
Salvation, rain and, 58
Scopes trial, 14, 70
Self-destruction, Brett and, 83–84
Self-mastery, development and,
  59–63

Self-pity, life and, 60–61
Sexuality
    ambiguity and, 81–85
    Brett and, 16, 64–65, 67–68
    Jake and, 16, 22, 24–25, 46–47
Sickness, Georgette and, 18–19
Steers, 35–36
Stein, Gertrude, 11, 14, 86, 90
Stewart, Donald Ogden, 69
Strether, Lambert (*The Ambassadors*), 88, 89, 92
Suffrage, influence of, 14
Suicide, 12
Surrogate, Pedro Romero as, 17

T

Taxis, intimacy and, 46–47
Toklas, Alice B., 86
Toronto Star, 11
The Torrents of Spring, 90
Travel, enjoyment of, 31–32
Truth, Hemingway and, 50–53
Twysden, Duff, 76–77

U

Uncertainty, 36, 42–43

V

Violence, degradation and, 54–57

Vionnet, Madame de (*The Ambassadors*), 90–91
Volstead Act, 20
Voting rights, influence of, 14

W

War, loss and, 20, 22, 27–28, 49–50, 61–62
Waste Land (Eliot)
    Bloom on, 7–8
    boredom and, 20
    inactivity and, 57–59
"The way it was", 50–53
When Lilacs Last in the Dooryard Bloom'd (Whitman), Bloom on, 7–8
Whitman, Walt, 7–8
Wine-skins, 37
Women
    Georgette and, 18–19
    Hemingway and, 28
    indestructibility of, 64–68
    stereotypes and, 83–84
    voting rights of, 14
World War I
    death of love and, 22
    effects of, 20